WINDOWS ON WIDOWHOOD

WINDOWS ON WIDOWHOOD

by
Jocelyn G Murray

GODALMING
SURREY

ADELAIDE
S. AUSTRALIA

First published in England in 1995 by Highland Books, Two High Pines, Knoll Road, Godalming, Surrey GU7 2EP

Published in Australia in 1995 by Openbook Publishers, 205 Halifax Street, South Australia 5000.

Library Cataloguing-in-Publication Data. A catalogue record for this book is available from the British Library.

Cover Design: Sally Maltby

ISBN: 1 897913 22 2

Printed in Great Britain by HarperCollins, Glasgow

Table Of Contents

Dedicated
to the
Glory of God

In memory of

Alan

loving husband, friend and father.
Without his life and death this book
could not have been written.

"Christ will be exalted in my body,
whether by life or by death. For to me,
to live is Christ and to die is gain"
Philippians 1:20-21

Acknowledgments

I owe a debt of gratitude to many who have contributed, in various ways, to enable this book to be written and published.

Firstly, I want to thank my children, Michelle, Rachel and Andrew, for their love and patience in allowing their mother the many hours needed for writing. I want to express my grateful thanks to my faithful friend and mentor, Stephanie Butel, for her tireless checking and re-checking of the manuscript from start to finish. Without her continued encouragement, wisdom and counsel I doubt whether this book would have reached your hands.

My grateful thanks to Beryl Anderson, Elaine Barnett and Jocelyn McKenzie, who took the time to read the manuscript and offer their constructive help.

A special thanks to my friend Lyn Flett for her expertise in correcting my often clumsy grammar. Many thanks to Anne Stevens for her help in setting up the manuscript ready for printing. Thanks to Ross Callighan for his invaluable assistance in showing me how to edit the manuscript.

Thanks to Janet Fleming and Kath Howan for permission to quote from their poems.

I am grateful to Joyce Huggett for her encouragement to persevere with my writing and her willingness to write the Foreword. Thank you to all those who have encouraged and prayed for me while writing this book.

Foreword

I met Jocelyn Murray on my first visit to New Zealand. When she told me her story: the sudden death of her husband, the nature of the research she was embarking on and her desire to write, I sensed that God was going to bring something rich from this sequence of events. He has – not least, in the form of this book.

When I read the manuscript, I found myself marvelling at the author's skill. On the one hand she has produced a thrilling meditation on the Book of Ruth which, like a bubbling stream, carries the reader along in its current. On the other hand, she has woven into the story reflections on the grieving process, drawing unashamedly from her own bitter-sweet experiences. The result is that the reader is left with a deeper understanding of the Scripture because the author has unearthed a variety of insights into the Book of Ruth which are not often highlighted these days. And, more importantly, the reader is left with a recurring refrain ringing in their ears: 'God is faithful'.

In underlining the faithfulness of the God who cares, Jocelyn Murray does not deny the pain of bereavement nor fall into the trap of suggesting that grief-work can be completed in a hurry. The book will therefore be of great value, I believe, to those who have lost loved ones. It will also help those of us who are called, from time to time, to come alongside the bereaved. From it we may glean glimpses of the pressures and heartaches that afflict those whose loved ones have died, particularly widows and widowers. It has been a very great privilege for me to read this manuscript and I count it an even greater privilege to be the one to write this Foreword and to give this book my warm commendation.

Joyce Huggett

Preface

Ward 3! It was true! This was the cancer ward. Nurses told us we had the best room in the hospital but instead of comforting us this only relayed more forcefully the seriousness of our situation.

Just an hour earlier we were stunned when our local doctor told us the result of Alan's blood test: "I have news that will be a shock to you both...you have leukaemia!" A shot of pain surged through my heart. I sat in the silence of numbed disbelief! The doctor continued to speak but I wasn't hearing. I looked at Alan sitting opposite me and saw him quickly brush aside large beads of sweat which had suddenly appeared on his forehead. My heart ached for him.

It was Friday 19th December 1986, the day Alan left the job he had worked at for twenty-three years to start a full-time Bible teaching ministry. What was God doing? This same day Alan was diagnosed with acute leukaemia, with a maximum life expectancy of two months! Although there was much prayer for Alan's healing by many Christians in churches throughout the land, God chose not to heal him. God chose instead to take Alan to be with Himself at 9.30 a.m. on 3rd April 1987.

During the long winter of 1987, I drew close to the Lord in my grief. My strength to go on came from Him. From within me came a strong desire to know the Lord better and to grow in my understanding of the Bible. This desire led me to embark on a course of study at Bible College. Because my children were still young I was only able to attend as a part-time student and finally graduated in 1994.

It was while writing an assignment on the life of Ruth that a seed was sown in my mind to write this book. I had received excellent marks and the lecturer had encouraged me to consider taking the subject further. My first approach was to write a manuscript on all the widows in the Bible. The chapter on Ruth and Naomi became the bones of this book but it has taken a further six years for the flesh to be added.

I have written in response to my own question: what does God have to say to the widow? I learnt that God never leaves us alone in our grief but stands beside us and grieves with us. I discovered that there is life beyond widowhood because God has a plan and purpose for our life that doesn't end with the death of our spouse. Recognition of this fact is the key to turning tragedy into triumph. The God who bothers to count the number of hairs on our head surely does have a plan and purpose for our life!

I learnt and experienced many of the insights and lessons portrayed in this book, while I was writing. My prayer is that as God has blessed me in writing, He will bless you in reading. I pray that you will also discover the reality of knowing and trusting God when He says that "...in all things God works for the good of those who love him" (Romans 8:28).

Jocelyn G Murray

Chapter 1

Widowed

'Widow', I hate that term! So said my diary eight weeks after Alan had died.

Earlier that day I had filled out a form which asked for my marital status. For the first time in nineteen years I couldn't put 'married'. As I reluctantly entered the word 'widow' there was a battle going on in my mind: aren't all widows old, poor, lonely, alone? *I'm too young to be widowed!* Didn't God say that the length of our days is seventy, or eighty years? Even statistics prove that most widows are over sixty-five!

Alan had died a few months after his forty-first birthday and now, here I was a widow with three young children. It just didn't seem right or fair.

How I hated that term 'widow'. How I cringed when I had to admit it on paper.

No-one wants to be widowed. The complete family unit is suddenly shattered. The unplanned and undesirable change of circumstances, takes a wife or husband from a place of security to uncertainty. The two, joined as one, are abruptly torn apart. The love, protection and intimate friendship is snatched away. You grieve for the loss of your partner. You feel so vulnerable.

I desperately wanted to know what God had to say about widows so I turned to my Bible and read through the fifth chapter of 1 Timothy. Perhaps there I would find some comfort. I was devastated! Once again I saw the widow in negative terms: morally, sexually and spiritually vulnerable. Just like me! My grief was raw and new.

Some days later I looked up all the references I could find about widows in the Bible. I was amazed to find so many! Filled with a sense of awe, I began to read of God's love and compassion toward widows. He demanded laws for their protection and provision of their daily needs in a society that down-graded women.

When I re-read 1 Timothy 5, it dawned on me that the apostle Paul was in fact, deeply concerned for the well-being of widows. He was anxious for the early believers to look after widows in their distress.

There was comfort for me from God's Word after all!

God's Compassion

As I studied these passages I became more intensely aware of the love and compassion of God. I was struck by the magnitude of God's love! The almighty God who created all things was not only deeply interested in what was happening to me but understood my feelings. He was with me in my grief and wanted to relieve my suffering.

I experienced again the incredible, overwhelming sense of God's love and compassion that had saturated my whole being just hours before Alan's death.

God had continually showered us with all sorts of blessings during Alan's fourteen weeks of illness. Even during the early hours of his last morning on earth I marvelled at God's care–His provision, without cost, of a private carpeted room in a hospital with full wards and the service of a Christian night nurse. Although we did not know her, she had heard of Alan's illness and had been praying for us.

These provisions showed the loving care of a compassionate God who is interested in all aspects of our suffering. Alan was unconscious, therefore God gave them to me as an expression of His love. He was displaying to me His deep feeling and understanding of my suffering. His desire was to alleviate my pain.

Alan was suffering from a massive cerebral haemorrhage due to his leukaemia. When the night doctor told me he only had two hours to live, I experienced a closeness of the Lord's presence which is almost impossible to describe.

It was as if the Lord, in person, had entered that hospital room and placed His arms of love around us both. I found myself humming, singing and praying.

I remember one song in particular... 'Jesus, Jesus, Jesus, your love has melted my heart'. I thought I should be singing something about heaven but these words about the love of Christ filled my mind.

God was impressing upon me, as He suffered with me, the assurance of His deep love. Despite the circumstances, He was in control. Gently, ever so gently, I felt the love of God enabling me to release my hold on Alan. In His strength I was able to ask the Lord to take him peacefully, without pain, into His presence.

As I walked out of the ward, God intervened again. Passing the hospital chapel I heard the singing of 'Amazing Grace.' It was Alan's favourite hymn!

Amazing grace, how sweet the sound,
that saved a wretch like me!
I once was lost, but now am found,
was blind but now I see.

God was reminding me that He had not abandoned me, even though He had taken Alan home to be with Himself. He was walking with me in my grief. I felt conscious of a deeper thankfulness for the gift of salvation. It was comforting to know that because Alan had accepted God's salvation, he was now face to face with his Saviour.

God in His compassion does not stand aloof from our suffering. He sympathises with our weaknesses. He suffers with us in our distress. Not only does God suffer with us but He wants to "... bind up the brokenhearted..."(Isa 61:1).

I can testify today, along with King David who made the claim some 900 years before Christ, that: "The Lord is compassionate and gracious. . . As a father has compassion on his children, so the Lord has compassion on those who fear Him" (Psalm 103:8,13).

He does heal the broken heart and bind up the wounds!

My vulnerability

While I was experiencing the incredible compassion of God I was also very, very vulnerable.

Six weeks into widowhood my diary reads: *I feel like I've been shattered into a hundred pieces and have to pick up the pieces one at a time to become whole again; like a piece of pottery dropped and shattered that will take time and patience to fix. Each piece hurts and aches as I hand it to the Father. . . I can't fix it, He does it for me.*

Like David, I cried out. . .

> "Be merciful to me, O Lord, for I am in distress;
> my eyes grow weak with sorrow,
> my soul and my body with grief. . .
> I have become like broken pottery"
>
> Psalm 31:9,12

I felt so vulnerable! Open to emotional and physical wounding. Little things would cause me to weep. . . driving past places where, as a couple, we had spent time together; sitting alone in church surrounded by friends with their partners; standing alone watching my son play his Saturday soccer match. I found it humbling to stand in a queue of unemployed and solo parents at Social Welfare in order to receive the widow's benefit.

I felt anger, self pity and frustration at having to provide a death certificate to the insurance company, Social Welfare and even the telephone company, to prove my husband was really dead!

At three months my diary reads: *I feel very vulnerable as a widow. Suddenly I realise how protected I was in marriage. Stripped of that protection, I feel quite alone with my feelings. I'm feeling threatened by the friendliness of a single man who has already given me a gift of money and has offered to pay my bills. He's not a Christian! He's divorced!*

Why couldn't I have just accepted his friendliness as a gesture of kindness and compassion? Simply because I felt vulnerable! I did not, at that time, have any set income and I was concerned about what he may expect in return. I no longer had the protection a husband provides.

Was God interested in my vulnerability? I knew he cared for me but did God really understand my social unease? Did he sense my emotional see-saw? I needed reassurance. I turned once more to my Bible and read the stories of widows in the Old Testament. I discovered that the social vulnerability of the widow in the ancient Middle East was much more extreme than mine.

It was a society which depended heavily on human muscle power for subsistence. A family composed of a widow and her children found it difficult to survive. If the widow had no adult male relative to act as her legal protector she was in danger of abuse and exploitation. With no insurance or social welfare system, she was in a precarious position.*

An awareness of these difficulties made me grateful for today's social welfare system in New Zealand. I could receive the support of the widow's benefit and I could also legally own property and maintain it, whether or not I had children.**

* Property was to be kept within the husband's family name therefore it appears that widows did not actually 'own' property (Deut 14:28,29; 25:5-10). If a widow had young children she would only be entrusted with the property until her son or daughter came of age. If the widow had an adult son, then he automatically inherited the property and she was cared for by him. If she had no sons then God's laws allowed an adult daughter to inherit the property. The daughter was only permitted to marry within the tribal clan of her father so that her heir would carry on the family name and inherit the land (Num 27:1-11; 36:1-12).

** If a widow in the ancient Middle East had no children then there was no heir to carry on the family name. There were several ways she could overcome this problem. She could remarry soon after her bereavement (Abigail and Bathsheba -1 Sam 25, 2 Sam 11); or return to her father's house (Tamar - Gen 38:11); or if her brother-in-law or another relative bought the property of the deceased, marriage could take place. The first-born son of this union would then inherit the deceased husband's property. This was known as a 'levirate'

Throughout the Old Testament there are repeated warnings against those who took advantage of the widow, defrauding her of civil rights and coveting her land. Widows who lived in that era needed constant protection from those who tried to mistreat, or take advantage of them.

The ancient Israelite society held the common view that widowhood was a 'reproach' from God. This caused widows to feel a sense of disgrace and public humiliation.

As I studied the Old Testament passages, I was delighted to find that God did not see widowhood as a reproach! Instead, he promised to defend, sustain, protect and provide for the widow. She was not to be deprived of justice, clothing or land.[1]

How were these promises of God accomplished? Did the Israelites sit back and leave God to fulfil his promises? No! God, who understands the vulnerability of the widow, gave the Israelites laws for her protection. For example, He gave three distinct laws for the provision of food.

First, at harvest time grain was to be left in the fields, olives were to be left on the trees and grapes on the vines so that the poor could gather sufficient to eat. (The 'poor' included widows, orphans and unemployed foreigners). Secondly, every third year a tithe of all produce was to be brought

marriage (Ruth-Dt 25:5-10, Rth 4:3-10).

to the local town to be distributed to the poor. In addition, every seventh year the land was to be left uncultivated, vines and trees unpruned and the poor were allowed to harvest whatever grew of itself during that year.[2]

God was very angry with those who didn't obey these laws. His punishments were many and varied. On some occasions, God inflicted the same situation upon the offenders.[3]

Boaz is a classic example of an Israelite who obeyed God's laws pertaining to widows. Rereading the book of Ruth, through widow's eyes, I gained new insight into the heart of love God has for the widow.

I discovered, like Ruth and Naomi did, that my identity was not to be found in my status or role as a widow, mother, secretary, wife or whatever but as a follower–a disciple of a loving God! Whatever my status, God has a plan and purpose for my ultimate good. He awaits my obedience.

The book of Ruth is a delightful piece of history. It reveals how a poor Moabite widow was accepted in Israel and came to be considered as better than seven sons! Obed, her son, became the grandfather of King David and therefore in the lineage of the King of Kings – Jesus Christ! God lifted Ruth from a life of social reproach to a place of honour.

Naomi, Ruth's widowed mother-in-law, also became a woman of influence because she allowed God to work through her for the blessing of others.

How did Ruth, a young destitute widow, come to be blessed beyond her wildest dreams? How did Naomi, an older widow who seemed to have no future, discover God's richest blessings in her latter years?

Let's take a closer look at this story. Let's discover how Ruth and Naomi became women of influence and how tragedy can be turned into triumph!

Why Lord? A young man in his prime,
Snatched from this earth before his time.
His talents Lord to You he'd bring,
His hands to strum, his voice to sing.
In faith the congregation prayed,
A pathway to Your throne they made.
They trusted You his life to raise,
And gave to You their fervent praise.
Oh Father, was their faith misplaced?
Were all their prayers simply a waste?
What lessons must they learn from this?
It seems Your perfect will they missed.

Another life once in His prime,
He came to earth in Your good time.
His life was far beyond compare,
And yet that life You did not spare.
His friends, all yearned for Him to stay,
But, "No," He said, "I must away.
The future's in my Father's hand,
I'm here to do as He has planned."
And so He died in pain and grief.
For Him there could be no relief.
So did He die before His time?
Oh Lord, this young man in His prime?

Oh no, His time had fully come.
He stood before His captors, dumb,
So He could do My perfect will,
And die upon Golgotha's Hill.
Your times are also in My hand,
And though you may not understand.
One day your eyes will truly see.
'Til then, have confidence in Me

'In His Time' by Kath Howan

In the days when the judges ruled, there was a famine in the land, and a man from Bethlehem in Judah, together with his wife and two sons, went to live for a while in the country of Moab.

The man's name was Elimelech, his wife's name Naomi, and the names of his two sons were Mahlon and Kilion. They were Ephrathites from Bethlehem, Judah. And they went to Moab and lived there.

Now Elimelech, Naomi's husband, died, and she was left with her two sons. They married Moabite women, one named Orpah and the other Ruth. After they had lived there about ten years, both Mahlon and Kilion also died, and Naomi was left without her two sons and her husband.

Ruth 1:1-5

Chapter 2

Why Me?

God's ways and thoughts stretch far beyond the realms of our human reasoning. We can't always understand why He allows suffering in our lives. Ruth and Naomi would never have known in their lifetime, the full extent of God's plans, purposes and blessing for them. However, because of their faithfulness and obedience to God, despite their circumstances, God was able to work through them to fulfil His promise to Abraham–to bless all nations of the earth through his seed (Gen 12:2-3).

It's exciting to know that God has also got a plan and purpose for our lives. No matter what our status, whether single, married or widowed, He wants us to trust and obey Him. We are to follow His ways as Ruth and Naomi did and He will work in us to fulfil His purposes.

In this story of Ruth we are not told why Naomi's husband, Elimelech and the family packed their bags and left Bethlehem for a temporary stay in the land of Moab. We are simply told that a famine swept over the land of Israel.

Elimelech was a worshipper of God* and may have thought the famine was a sign of God's anger at the spiritual apathy and apostasy that reigned throughout Bethlehem.

A quick look through the book of Judges reveals the sad condition of God's people at this time. God repeatedly says, "The Israelites did evil in the eyes of the Lord." Elimelech probably considered that living in Moab with its pagan practices wouldn't be any different! Perhaps life would even be better–at least his family would have food!

Whatever Elimelech's reasons were for moving to the fertile plains of Moab, he no doubt thought of the physical welfare of his wife and sons. The temporary stay that Elimelech had envisaged however, stretched out into at least ten years.

Death–Why, God?

Death–the very thing Elimelech had hoped to avoid by moving to Moab, struck their home. Not

* To the Hebrew mind, to know a person's name is to know his character. From the meaning of Elimelech's name and the subsequent story of Naomi it is obvious they loved and worshipped God. Elimelech meaning 'My God is King' and Naomi meaning 'pleasant, lovely, delightful', were the parents of two sons–Mahlon meaning 'sick' and Kilion meaning 'wasting away', or 'pining'. [4]

once, but three times. Elimelech himself died, leaving Naomi a widow in a foreign land. This was followed by the death of their two sons who had married Moabite wives.

- The complete family unit shattered.
- The two joined as one–torn apart.
- The love, protection and intimate friendship–snatched away.

The Bible narrator is silent concerning the reasons behind the tragic deaths of all the males in this Israelite home, yet there have been many suggestions throughout the centuries as to why they occurred.

Too often, like Job's comforters, we try to reason why God allows certain circumstances to occur in our lives but Job was not told why God tested him. He learnt that people by themselves, cannot find out the reason why anyone suffers unless God wishes to reveal it to them.

When Job questioned his suffering, God answered by reminding him of the wonders of His creative power. He then asked Job, "Who has a claim against me that I must pay? Everything under heaven belongs to me" (Job 41:11). Humbled before His creator Job exclaimed, "I know that you can do all things; no plan of yours can be thwarted" (Job 42:2). He had gained a new understanding and appreciation of his God.

Like Job, I asked the question "Why, God?" On receiving no clear answer I have had to bow to a sovereign God who makes no mistakes.

It is not wrong to ask this question! It was reassuring to me when questioning, to remember that even Christ–in His humanity–while suffering on the cross, asked His Father:

"My God, My God why have you forsaken me?" (Matt 27:46)

My faith tested

I found it helpful to think about Job's testing. In the first two chapters of the book of Job we are told that God allowed Satan to test him. The angels in heaven watched to see SatanÕs testing and Job's reaction. They saw the humiliation of Satan and the proof of Job's devotion. It was pure and his faith was genuine. Job declared, "But he knows the way I take; when he has tested me, I will come forth as gold" (Job 23:10). This statement is proof of Job's remarkable faith in God. He truly believed God would eventually turn his suffering into good.

In the New Testament, we are reminded that angels watch to see how we endure "all kinds of trials", so that our "faith. . . may be proved genuine" (1 Peter 1:6,7;1 Cor 4:9).

We cannot always understand the ways of God and God does not always wish to reveal them to us. Job's suffering was not a punishment for sin. Job could never fathom his suffering but it accomplished God's higher purposes for him. "For my thoughts are not your thoughts, neither are your ways my ways, declares the Lord. . . my ways are higher than your ways and my thoughts than your thoughts" (Isaiah 55:8,9). When God had achieved his higher purposes through Job, He made him prosperous again and gave him twice as much as he had before.

Like Job, who was never told the reason for his testings, Ruth and Naomi never learnt the reason for their husbands' deaths. They never understood why God allowed these tragedies to occur. Their faith was severely tested, yet through their suffering they came to a deeper understanding and appreciation of God. They humbly yielded to Him, trusting that He would continue to love, guide and protect them, despite their sad circumstances.

When I yielded to God's sovereignty, I stopped struggling to find a reason for Alan's death. My struggling was replaced with the peace of God which passes all understanding. This peace enabled me to trust Him, without understanding the reasons.

Why do the righteous suffer?

From the narrative of Job I learnt the difference between the suffering of the wicked as punishment and the suffering of the righteous to accomplish God's higher purposes.[5] In the narrative of Ruth there is no mention of Ruth or Naomi suffering because of some wickedness. Instead, it is the righteousness of the three main characters that is continually brought to the reader's attention.

After the bereaved have asked the question, "Why has this happened to me?" often the next question is, "What have I done to deserve this; what sin am I guilty of?" as if trying to find an answer to the first question.

Although it is natural to ask these questions, if we do, we are forgetting God's sovereign right to take life when and how He chooses (John 21:19-23). We are forgetting that in God's sight, the death of his saints is precious (Ps 116:15). We are forgetting that it is Jesus' desire to have the believer with Him in glory (John 17:24). We must remember that God has a higher purpose which we cannot fathom (Isa 55:8,9). In our distress, we lament our position even more if we do not remember God's sovereignty over our lives.

One Sunday morning about four months after Alan's death, I was encouraged by an address given by a visiting speaker to my church. He spoke on the life of King Jotham who was righteous in his walk and work for the Lord and yet he died at the early age of forty-one.

I was struck with the parallels in Jotham and Alan's lives. Jotham "did what was right in the eyes of the Lord," and ". . . walked steadfastly before the Lord his God. . . " (2 Chr 27:2,6).

Alan had always sought to do what was right in the eyes of the Lord and was faithful in his walk before the Lord, yet he also died at the same age.

Jotham did not die because of some sin he had committed. Rather, it is recorded he lived righteously. God tells us: "a righteous man will be remembered forever" (Ps 112:6). And those who fear the Lord and talk with each other about Him are recorded in His "scroll of remembrance" (Mal 3:16).

In the story of Job, we see that God never accused him of any sin. Instead, we read that God said to Satan concerning Job, ". . . you incited me against him to ruin him without any reason" (Job 2:3). The translation of this Hebrew word 'hinnam' as "without any reason" is good at this point, because it means that 'there was no immediate sinfulness in Job that called for punishment'.[6]

Likewise in the story of Ruth, God does not accuse or condemn Naomi or Elimelech, Ruth or Mahlon, Orpah or Kilion of any sin. Neither does the narrator. However earlier Jewish writers, along with some later commentators, have judged the deaths of the males in this family as a result of sin. They suggest it is because they left God's people in Bethlehem or because the sons married Moabite wives.

It is wise to take notice of the narrator's silence in both stories and see God's dealings with the righteous to accomplish His higher purposes.

For some reason there are always people like Job's friends, who condemn and judge sickness or death of another Christian as a sign of God's judgment. Do they have the right to judge? God was certainly not enchanted by Job's comforters!

During the fourteen weeks of Alan's illness we experienced an amazing outpouring of love from Christians throughout New Zealand. Special prayer meetings were arranged to ask for God's healing and to pray for the extra strength that I needed. Every day there would be letters of encouragement, phone enquiries, meals cooked, gifts of baking, boxes of food and gifts of money. These gifts overwhelmed us. We were greatly humbled in gratitude before the Lord. The supply of food was so abundant that I literally did not have enough room in the cupboards, even though I have a large kitchen with plenty of cupboard space! The verse in Malachi 3:10 became a living reality for us: "Test me in this," says the Lord Almighty, "and see if I will not throw open the floodgates of heaven and pour out so much blessing that you will not have room enough for it."

These expressions of love were received not only from those who knew us very well but also from those who had only heard of Alan's illness and knew of his love for the Lord. Yet, amidst all these blessings lavished upon us by God, we suffered the injustice of false accusations. One friend thought it necessary to tell me about some injustice Alan was alleged to have committed. For my benefit, it was expressed, "Alan's not as perfect as you think!" This caused unnecessary hurt and heartache at a time when I badly needed support and encouragement. Some years later when I confronted this friend with the issue, there were apologies and an admission that the accusations had proved to be false.

We do well not to judge God's action in permitting suffering in another Christian's life. Instead, we are told to pray, help and love one another. It would have been wiser if our friend had kept silent and quietly acknowledged that God has a purpose in the suffering of the righteous.

God does not promise that the Christian will be free from suffering. David reminds us in Psalm 34:19: "A righteous man may have many troubles, but the Lord delivers him from them all." John also reminds us that suffering occurs so that the work of God might be displayed in our lives. This results in bringing praise, glory and honour to God (John 9:3 cf 1 Peter 1:7).

The examples of Job, Ruth and Naomi show us that God permits circumstances, whether good or bad, to occur in our lives to achieve His own purposes. They had the freedom to accept or reject God's plans but humble submission was required to be part of that plan. Jesus is the supreme example of one who suffered in order to fulfil God's higher purposes and bring glory to His Father. . .

> "During the days of Jesus' life on earth, he offered up prayers and petitions with loud cries and tears to the one who could save him from death, and he was heard because of his reverent submission. Although he was a son, he learned obedience from what he suffered. . ."
>
> Hebrews 5:7,8

Faith in God's sovereignty

Faith in the sovereignty of God, or to use a simpler term, Lordship of God, makes the difference between accepting suffering or becoming bitter. It's necessary to learn to trust God's sovereign will for us even when all our human reasonings lead us to a different conclusion.

Although I still cannot understand why God chose to take Alan to be with Himself at such an early age, I have learned to bow and accept His sovereign ways. When I was struggling to come to terms with this, the Lord impressed upon me two particular passages of Scripture.

In answer to my question as to whether I could have done anything different to prolong Alan's life, the Lord reminded me that we can do nothing to prolong life! The number of days a person lives are already determined by God. His Word says, "Man's days are determined; you have decreed the number of his months and have set limits he cannot exceed" (Job 14:5).

The second passage of Scripture which comforted me was John 21:18-23. I was stunned to realise that Jesus told Peter how he would die and the reason why he would die in this particular way. It was to bring glory to God: "Jesus said this to indicate the kind of death by which Peter would glorify God." Like me, Peter was also stunned by this revelation. He turned and seeing John, pointed to him and asked, "Lord, what about him?" Jesus answered, "If I want him to remain alive until I return, what is that to you? You must follow me."

Jesus impressed upon Peter that it is His divine prerogative and sovereign right to take life when and how He wills. Also that it is He who determines the kind of death which will best bring glory to Himself. Paul, knowing this truth wrote: "I eagerly expect and hope that I... will have sufficient courage so that now as always Christ will be exalted in my body, whether by life or by death" (Phil 1:20).

Let me illustrate how this transpired for Alan, by quoting from extracts of letters sent to me after his death. These were written by friends who visited him during his illness:

> 'While reading through 2 Corinthians 4:16 "Though outwardly we are wasting away, yet inwardly we are being renewed day by day. For our light and momentary troubles are achieving for us an eternal glory that far outweighs them all", my thoughts turned to Alan and how much these verses were like him for as he got weaker and weaker physically, he became stronger and more like the Lord.'
>
> Paul

> 'Alan taught me many lessons as I watched him deteriorate physically but continue to mature spiritually. That faith, that peace, that confidence he had in God never wavered. Although obviously concerned about the possibility of leaving his family and friends, his words remained the same, "God is all-knowing, He knows the beginning from the end, He knows the best for all; I will trust Him to the end knowing that He will do what is right and best."
>
> These words may sound feeble to some, but to those who knew Alan, who knew how well he knew God, through his Christian experience, and amazing knowledge of the Bible, these words were truth and reality.

Alan's life and death have both had a big impact on my life, and I want to quote the Word of God which Alan loved so much, "Through his faith Abel won God's approval as a righteous man, because God himself approved of his gifts. By means of his death Abel still speaks, even though he is dead" (Heb 11:4). I am confident that this verse is also true of Alan.'

Des

'In the home I found a sense of calm and peace and a positive trusting in the Lord. An acceptance that things were in the Lord's hands. Coming as an encourager, I was the one who came away encouraged. I was challenged and impressed by the quiet confidence that Alan always displayed in His God.'

Warren

It was also a time of witnessing to those who did not know God. The cancer specialist, who came to know Alan well during his short illness, entered his hospital room one day and in a burst of anger and frustration exclaimed,

"You can express your anger if you want to. You don't always have to look happy!"

This opportunity was not to be missed by Alan, who replied calmly, "Well doctor, whether I live or die I belong to the Lord."

The doctor, looking a little amazed replied, "I wish I could have that kind of faith."

Alan was quick to tell him that anyone could experience this faith and added with his touch of Scottish humour, "What's more doctor, it's free!"

One nurse turned to me when outside his room, and said, "Your husband is different from others we have in this ward. What is it? Why is he able to be so cheerful?" This gave me an opportunity to testify that Alan's confidence was founded in God.

Nell Collins, a Christian nurse, sums it up this way…

> 'God leaves us here after we become his to bring glory to his name in special ways–ways that he chooses. Now one person might glorify him from a sickbed. Another person may bring glory to him while dying from cancer. Someone else may glorify him with extra good health or tremendous riches. The point is that we do not tell God which way we choose to glorify him. We accept his way, and then we begin to see how he can use for his glory something that seems like a tragedy to us'[7]

As well as bringing glory to God, Paul reminds us that "our light and momentary troubles are achieving for us an eternal glory that far outweighs them all" (2 Cor 4:17). I can't comprehend the depth of meaning in this verse. However, nine months after Alan's death, when trying to make some rhyme and reason of my circumstances, I pondered over this verse and wrote in my diary: earthly suffering for Christ's sake adds to the dimension of a person's ability to appreciate the glory of God for eternity.

> "And we, who with unveiled faces all reflect the Lord's glory, are being transformed into his likeness with ever-increasing glory..."
>
> 2 Cor 3:18

When she heard in Moab that the Lord had come to the aid of his people by providing food for them, Naomi and her daughters-in-law prepared to return home from there. With her two daughters-in-law she left the place where she had been living and set out on the road that would take them back to the land of Judah.

Then Naomi said to her two daughters-in-law, "Go back, each of you, to your mother's home. May the Lord show kindness to you, as you have shown to your dead and to me. May the Lord grant that each of you will find rest in the home of another husband." Then she kissed them and they wept aloud and said to her, "We will go back with you to your people."

But Naomi said, "Return home, my daughters. Why would you come with me? Am I going to have any more sons, who could become your husbands? Return home my daughters; I am too old to have another husband. Even if I thought there was still hope for me–even if I had a husband tonight and then gave birth to sons–would you wait until they grew up? Would you remain unmarried for them? No, my daughters. It is more bitter for me than for you, because the Lord's hand has gone out against me!" At this they wept again. Then Orpah kissed her mother-in-law goodbye, but Ruth clung to her.

"Look", said Naomi, "your sister-in-law is going back to her people and her gods. Go back with her."

But Ruth replied, "Don't urge me to leave you or to turn back from you. Where you go I will go, and where you stay I will stay. Your people will be my people and your God my God. Where you die I will die, and there I will be buried. May the Lord deal with me, be it ever so severely, if anything but death separates you and me."

When Naomi realized that Ruth was determined to go with her, she stopped urging her.

Ruth 1:6-18

Chapter 3

Identity Crisis

The death of my husband shook the very roots of my life. Suddenly stripped of my identity as a wife, I stood on my own without the support and love of my husband. It was a time of asking myself many questions:

Once a wife, now a widow. Is that all I am?

Am I a 'single' again, as well?

Is my identity to be based on my role in life

or me as a person?

Am I the same person?

I wanted to know exactly where my identity lay. One of the problems in our Western society is that we are inclined to evaluate others by their role rather than by who they are. When introduced to someone for the first time, invariably the first question asked is,"What do you do?" or "Where do you work?"

How does God evaluate us? He wants us to see ourselves as belonging to Him. We need to ask ourselves, "Who am I in Christ?" He wants us to find our identity as being complete in Him. With this knowledge we will be able to live for Him. It is easy to make the mistake of putting the cart before the horse. Our role is to flow from our identity in Christ and not from our role in life.

How did Ruth and Naomi overcome this identity crisis? How did these two destitute widows become women of influence for their God? It began when Naomi made the decision to return to Bethlehem. She believed the end of the famine was a sign of God's blessing once more resting upon Israel.

Naomi, Ruth and Orpah packed up their possessions and set out on the long and dangerous journey to Bethlehem. They had not gone far when Naomi stopped and encouraged Ruth and Orpah to go back to Moab.

It was not the dangers of the journey that caused Naomi to stop in her tracks. Nor was it the fear that her Moabite daughters-in-law may not be accepted in Bethlehem. Naomi loved Ruth and Orpah and desired the best for them, but in her grief and state of hopelessness, she could see no future for them in Bethlehem. Elimelech's property would not be hers to keep because she had no son to inherit it. Even if she remarried, she was too old to bear any more sons. The situation was bleak! What could she offer them?

Naomi was concerned about Ruth and Orpah's future. She prayed that God in His kindness would provide husbands for them in the land of Moab. Naomi was not only thinking of their need for protection and security but she was anxious that they restore their social status. In the ancient

Middle East, social status was gained through remarriage and the birth of sons.

Our reactions to death

Orpah followed Naomi with probably every intention of staying with her and Naomi thanked her for her kindness. However when Naomi suggested she return to Moab, Orpah wept, kissed Naomi then left her. Orpah chose to return to Moab and to "her gods" and that is the last we hear of her.

Previously, Orpah had been happily married and had enjoyed life in Moab as part of Naomi's household. When adversity had come however, it seems Orpah had no depth of love for the God of Israel. Perhaps her love had been centred in the frail things of this life. Like the parable of the seed sown in shallow soil that withered and died under the hot sun of adversity, Orpah's faith was tested and found wanting.

Ruth decided not to return to Moab. Instead she"clung" to Naomi. Unlike Orpah, she had come to a deeper understanding and appreciation of the God of Israel. In her decision to follow Naomi it is evident she put the God of Israel before others: "Your people will be my people, and your God my God." She earnestly sought to do what was right in the sight of God. I believe Ruth and Orpah's decisions were based on their understanding and appreciation of God.

While both women had lived with their husbands in the love and security of a God-fearing Israelite home they probably had not needed to question where their love was founded. They had been content to rest and rely on the faith of their husbands and in-laws. Widowhood abruptly caused them to have to re-evaluate their personal faith. Each had to question where their love was centred.

Widowhood tests whether or not our faith is genuine (1 Peter 1:6-7). Some widows will find, like Orpah, that their love has been centred in earthly things with no real commitment to God. Others, like Ruth, who have their love and trust firmly grounded in God, will find that this time of personal testing will strengthen their faith. As they draw closer into God for comfort and strength , this will cause a strengthening of their relationship with God and a deeper awareness and appreciation of the love of God. This results in a fuller commitment to a sovereign God who is working in us to accomplish His purposes.

Reflecting on my own situation, I can truthfully say that throughout the time of Alan's illness and death, I never once doubted the love of God or my love for Him. I did however, gain a deeper appreciation of the love of God in providing the gift of salvation. I was intensely grateful for the assurance that Alan was eternally with Christ and that I also shared in that inheritance.

For several months after Alan's death I experienced waves of fear that I did not know the Bible as well as I should. I had tended to ask Alan to give me the answer to a Bible query because I knew he would be able to answer with the appropriate verses.

There was nothing wrong with asking my husband these questions, but what I hadn't realised, was that I had become dependent upon Alan's knowledge of the Scriptures and not my own. Even though I was involved in leading several women's study groups and teaching Bible in Schools, I hadn't really been getting into any personal in-depth study for some years.

Some nights I would picture myself as having died instead of Alan. Face to face with the Lord I would hear Him ask me, *"Have you never read?"* This was the question Jesus had repeatedly asked the religious leaders when He was on earth! This caused me to read the Bible with a renewed hunger. Sometimes I would read whole books in a day or at least large portions of a book. I attended Bible College to develop skills of research. I developed a far deeper understanding of how God personally desires and delights to answer my questions from His Word.

My faith had definitely been genuine but I had to re-evaluate the depth of my relationship with God.

It has taken me years to stop thinking of myself in terms of my status as a 'widow' or as a 'single'. I had to learn that my complete identity was to be found in Christ; that as His 'disciple', I am one in whom He delights to accomplish His purposes. For me, this has been a process of first coming to terms with not being a wife but a widow and secondly of seeing myself as single again, even though I have three children. I eventually realised that my true identity didn't lie in either of these states but only in being a disciple of Christ.

Katie Wiebe in her book *Alone* describes widowhood as a psychological state and a term used in business and legal documents but not a lifelong sentence. She states that what God expected of her as a wife with a husband and four children, is the same as what He expected of her as a widow with four children–discipleship! [8]

Because Ruth placed herself totally in the hands of the living God and put her trust in Him, she lived above her circumstances. She found her identity in the God of Israel and was intent on following His people and His ways. In her vow Ruth was accepting God's sovereignty over her life and in doing so found a key to turning her tragedy into triumph. This was her first step towards becoming a woman of influence for God.

Naomi got a little more bogged down with her immediate circumstances and displayed all the classic stages of grief. As she gradually realised that her identity was to be found in God and not in her status, she also became a woman of influence for Him.

God loves to see us come to this place of quiet surrender. He desires of us a total commitment to Himself. God wants us to realise that despite adverse circumstances which may surround us, He has a plan and purpose for our good. He wants us to find that key to turn our tragedy into triumph.

He wants us to become women of influence for Him.

> "Commit your way to the Lord;
> Trust in him and he will do this:
> He will make your righteousness shine
> like the dawn, the justice of your cause
> like the noonday sun"
>
> Psalm 37:5,6

So the two women went on until they came to Bethehem. When they arrived in Bethlehem, the whole town was stirred because of them, and the women exclaimed, "Can this be Naomi?"

"Don't call me Naomi," she told them. "Call me Mara, because the Almighty has made my life very bitter. I went away full but the Lord has brought me back empty. Why call me Naomi? The Lord has afflicted me; the Almighty has brought misfortune upon me."

So Naomi returned from Moab accompanied by Ruth the Moabitess, her daughter-in-law, arriving in Bethlehem as the barley harvest was beginning.

Ruth 1:19-22

Chapter 4

It is Right to Grieve

After a long and dangerous journey the two weary, destitute widows arrived in Bethlehem. The town hummed with the news of their arrival. Naomi's appearance reflected the harsh experiences of life she had endured in Moab. When confronted by her old friends, she heard them whisper to each other, "Can this really be Naomi?"

Angrily Naomi replied with bitter irony, "Don't call me Naomi" (meaning pleasant, sweet) "but call me Mara" (meaning bitter).

Naomi was distraught with grief and bitterness. She cried out a lament to God, accusing Him of bringing her back to Bethlehem "empty".

This lament appears to be a self-pitying description of Naomi's afflictions where she blames God for her misfortunes. However, when I looked at studies done on laments in the Old Testament, I discovered two important things. First, that the function of the lament is to appeal to God's compassion. Secondly, that implicit in the cry of lament is the belief that God hears and is able to deliver the plaintiff out of deep trouble.[9]

Job made a similar lament before God when he couldn't comprehend why he was suffering so many misfortunes: "the Almighty, who has made me taste bitterness of soul" (Job 27:2). Like Naomi, he held on to a God he could no longer understand, yet one whom he believed was faithful and compassionate! When there was no logical explanation for their suffering they put their trust in the *character* of God.

The prophet Isaiah reminds us that God longs to be gracious and show compassion to those who turn to Him for comfort and relief. "How gracious he will be when you cry for help! As soon as he hears, he will answer you" (Isaiah 30:19).

Those of us who have suffered the loss of a spouse or child will understand Naomi's frustration and anguish, as we recall experiencing similar feelings.

I remember during the early weeks of grief feeling particularly low after a day of fixing up legal matters. I couldn't sleep. After spending some hours weeping, I got up at two in the morning to make myself a hot drink. While sitting at the dining table sipping Milo, my attention was drawn to a picture of a beautiful sunset which hung above the china cabinet. Through my tears I read the words printed along the bottom:

> "Your love, O Lord, reaches to the heavens,
> your faithfulness to the skies"
>
> Psalm 36:5

As I thought about these words, I was reminded of God's character of love and faithfulness. I started to think about His everlasting, sustaining love that bridged the gap between earth and heaven at the cross. The more I thought about His love, the more I was encouraged. It was the same love that was holding on to me! I reached out in faith simply trusting in His love and faithfulness.

The endurance of faith required by a child of God through the bitter pain of bereavement is stretched to the maximum. However, through this testing God strengthens the faith of those who trust in the character of God.

It is not necessarily true that one will feel all the emotions of anxiety, anger, guilt, resentment and depression that Naomi displayed. Some doctors will even tell the bereaved they 'must' work through all these emotions. We should not feel as if we're not grieving correctly if we have not gone through this process! I did not feel any anger or guilt. This was because I was seeing God's continual blessing upon us throughout Alan's illness and death. I did however, experience days when I resented the fact that Alan's life had been cut-off at an early age. This caused me to ask God, "Why?" I had fluctuating feelings of anxiety about the future. I had days when I felt depressed. Yet, praise God, He always delivered me out of that state.

By faith, we must accept that God's plans and purposes for us will sometimes include circumstances we cannot comprehend. We can either accept this or reject it. Rejection will cause us to become bitter. If we accept it, believing that God has an overall plan for our ultimate good, we will grow through the experience. We will develop a closer relationship with God.

How did Ruth live above her circumstances? In her vow to Naomi she placed herself totally in the hands of God. This meant her identity was based in her relationship with God. She explicitly acknowledged God's sovereignty over her life. I believe it is because Ruth readily accepted this fundamental fact that she was able to live above her circumstances. In the same way, if we recognise our position in Christ as His disciple and accept God's sovereignty in our lives, we will be able to rise above adverse circumstances.

It should not be thought that Ruth did not grieve. Along with Naomi, she wore the customary garment of a widow, which was a dark textured cloth known as sackcloth. She also abstained from personal anointing. Such abstention was seen as a sign of mourning.[10] This is indicated in Naomi's later instruction to Ruth to wash, anoint herself and put on her best clothes when she prepared to go to the threshing floor. Ruth also grieved as she wept aloud with Naomi and Orpah. This is a natural and normal reaction in grief. It releases tension and has a healing and soothing effect.

Tears

Too often in today's society weeping is looked upon as a weakness. Because of this the mourner hides his or her tears and feels compelled to weep alone.

Sir Alexander Fleming, the British bacteriologist and discoverer of penicillin, undertook a study of the chemical analysis of tears. The results revealed that tears contain an enzyme called Lysozyme which dissolves the outer coat of many bacteria.[11] Our Creator has placed in our bodies this natural provision for release of tension and grief. This is for our physical and emotional good. If we hide our feelings and pretend they are not there, this natural provision is suppressed and we may suffer emotional and physical consequences.

It is good to remind ourselves that many Bible characters wept. The prophet Jeremiah is known as 'the weeping prophet', Elisha wept, Joseph wept and David wept many times.[12] Paul often prayed with tears for the saints. The Lord himself wept over Jerusalem and again at the tomb of his friend Lazarus. "During the days of Jesus' life on earth, he offered up prayers and petitions with loud cries and tears to the one who could save him from death" (Heb 5:7).

Thank God for the gift of tears. When the Bible speaks of widows not being able to weep, it was a fate God allotted to the wicked.[13] It is right to weep and mourn at the parting of a loved one. It is true that the sting of death is removed but the pain of parting is not. The writer of Ecclesiastes states that there is "a time to weep and a time to laugh, a time to mourn and a time to dance" (Eccl 3:4). Paul reminded Christians in Romans 12:15 that he expected them to weep with those that mourn.

In the ancient Middle East mourners would catch their tears in wineskins and place them at the tombs of their loved ones. This is what David must have had in mind when he wrote in Psalm 56:8, "Record my lament; list my tears on your scroll (or 'put my tears in your wineskin' NIV note) are they not in your record?" What an amazing thing! The Almighty God who created the whole universe bothers to measure our tears in His wineskin and records in His scroll why we weep.[14]

If we have set our heart on following Christ as His disciple there is a promise of special blessing as we pass through this valley of tears...

> "Blessed are those whose strength is in you,
> who have set their hearts on pilgrimage.
> As they pass through the Valley of Baca
> (lit. tears) they make it a place of springs
> (new life); the autumn rains also cover it
> with pools (blessings). They go from strength
> to strength"
>
> Psalm 84:5-7

It is good to meditate on this promise. It is while in our weakness, in "the valley of Baca", that we will find new life if we draw strength from the Lord. He is the one who makes us strong when we are weak (2 Cor 12:9).

Our compassionate God desires to...

> "comfort all who mourn, and provide for those
> who grieve... To bestow on them a crown of
> beauty instead of ashes, the oil of gladness
> instead of mourning, and a garment of praise
> instead of a spirit of despair"
>
> Isaiah 61:2,3

Just as in the Old Testament lament of affliction, so too we are encouraged to approach God with confidence. Hebrews 4 tells us to pray to God as our great High Priest; to come and lay all our trials and sufferings before Him. Jesus did this when He was on earth! He cried out with tears to His Father. When we do this, the promise is that we will be strengthened and receive "grace to help us in our time of need" (Heb 4:16).

Although Ruth and Naomi expressed their grief differently, Ruth avoided the depression and anger that Naomi experienced by focusing on God. She found her identity in Him and sought to please Him. It was an upward and outward look.

Naomi took longer in coming to terms with her grief. Her identity as wife, mother and homemaker were all destroyed. She was an older widow with no prospects for the future. She had to reassess her relationship with God. She had to relearn that her true value was to be found in God.

Neither Ruth nor Naomi were wrong in the way they grieved. Neither were condemned by God. Naomi's lament was not sinful. It was a form of prayer because implicit in her lament was the belief that God would deliver her. As we read on we see how God delighted in delivering Naomi from her grief.

Praise God! His desire is to deliver us from our grief and bring us into a place of blessing.

> "When the Lord saw her, his heart went out to her and he said 'Don't cry'"
>
> Luke 7:13

> "You do not realize now what I am doing, but later you will understand"
>
> John 13:7

Now Naomi had a relative on her husband's side, from the clan of Elimelech, a man of standing, whose name was Boaz. And Ruth the Moabitess said to Naomi, "Let me go to the fields and pick up the leftover grain behind anyone in whose eyes I find favor."

Naomi said to her, "Go ahead, my daughter." So she went out and began to glean in the fields behind the harvesters. As it turned out, she found herself working in a field belonging to Boaz, who was from the clan of Elimelech. Just then Boaz arrived from Bethlehem and greeted the harvesters, "The Lord be with you!" "The Lord bless you!" they called back. Boaz asked the foreman of his harvesters, "Whose young woman is that?"

The foreman replied, "She is the Moabitess who came back from Moab with Naomi." She said, 'Please let me glean and gather among the sheaves behind the harvesters.' She went into the field and has worked steadily from morning till now, except for a short rest in the shelter.

So Boaz said to Ruth, "My daughter, listen to me. Don't go and glean in another field and don't go away from here. Stay here with my servant girls.Watch the field where the men are harvesting ,and follow along after the girls. I have told the men not to touch you. And whenever you are thirsty, go and get a drink from the water jars the men have filled." At this she bowed down with her face to the ground. She exclaimed, "Why have I found such favor in your eyes that you notice me–a foreigner?"

Boaz replied, "I've been told all about what you have done for your mother-in-law since the death of your husband–how you left your father and mother and your homeland and came to live with a people you did not know before. May the Lord repay you for what you have done. May you be richly rewarded by the Lord, the God of Israel, under whose wings you have come to take refuge."

"May I continue to find favor in your eyes, my lord," she said. "You have given me comfort and have spoken kindly to your servant, though I do not have the standing of one of your servant girls."

Ruth 2:1-13

Chapter 5

God Cares

It is easy to acknowledge God's care when all is going well in our lives but we often struggle when faced with difficulties and disappointments. These are the times when we have a greater need to know that God loves and cares for us.

The overwhelming love of God that I experienced at the time of Alan's death, strengthened and comforted me. It assured me that God really cared about me. I knew that His heart had gone out to me just as Jesus' heart had gone out to the widow of Nain in Luke 7:13. God has never stopped showing me that same compassion.

One example of God's amazing love occurred about three weeks after Alan's death. We decided to spend the Easter holidays with my sister and family at Wanganui and enjoyed a day at a nearby pine forest, collecting pine cones and tobogganing. Later that night I discovered that Alan's wedding ring, which I had been wearing on my right hand, was missing. I had chosen to wear the ring because at this early stage of grief, it made me feel as if I still had part of Alan with me. I wept and prayed. Although it was a little thing, it was precious to me. I reasoned with the Lord, "You know exactly where the ring is Lord therefore I know you are able to show us where to find it." I knew He understood my hurt but wondered if He would bother with such a minor thing.

The next day we all prayed before setting out to search for the ring. It seemed an impossible task because the previous day I had tramped over the entire forest collecting pine cones. We lined up, three adults and seven children. Looking like a police search party, we shuffled through the pine needles that carpeted the forest floor. It was worse than looking for a needle in a haystack!

Our combing of the forest was unsuccessful. Just when I was feeling it was hopeless and only giving a cursory look in the grass where the car had been parked, suddenly there was a yell of delight from my daughter Michelle. "I've found it!" She had decided to relook over an area where we had been tobogganing. Down on her knees and moving the pine needles with her hands, she had unearthed the ring. We hugged and cried together and praised God for this miracle of God's loving care.

Experiences for our good

When I lost the ring I was devastated. I could see no good in the situation but God allowed it to happen in order to show me just how much He cared. I learnt that God cared and knew about the little things in life that upset me, just as much as the major traumas. I learnt that God often allows difficulties in our lives to show us more of Himself. This draws us into a deeper relationship with Him.

God is always active on our behalf but we often don't appreciate or understand this until some time later. It may be months or even years later, when reflecting upon adverse experiences, that we realise God has been active for our good.

Naomi could not understand why God allowed her husband and sons to die. When greeting her old friends she was angry and bitter at God because of her changed circumstances.

Blinded by grief she was unable to see that through the experience she was being brought into a much deeper relationship with God. It was some time later, when reflecting on Ruth's day in the harvest field, that Naomi began to realise that God had not abandoned her.

With a sad heart Naomi turned to walk along the familiar path to the home she had once shared with Elimilech and her two sons. The empty and derelict house only served to highlight her own emptiness. Life for Naomi appeared to have lost its meaning and become purposeless.

Dr Richard Turnbull writing on the different stages of grief states:

> 'Once the intense pangs of grief are past their peak the bereaved person moves into a stage of apathy and depression and may adopt a submissive, defeated attitude... During the stage of depression the bereaved person may feel inadequate, tense, irritable and physically tired... Life appears to have lost its meaning and become purposeless'.[15]

This helps us understand Naomi's state of depression. Some of us will recall experiencing similar feelings at this stage of grief. God however, was eagerly waiting to show His love to Naomi.

As the story unfolds, we see how much He cares for Naomi and Ruth by filling their emptiness with good. The good was beyond Naomi's comprehension at this stage. Naomi was unaware that she had a wealthy relative nearby who owned property. The narrator however, wants us to be aware of this information so that when Ruth and Boaz meet, in what seems to be a pure coincidence, we know that God was behind their encounter.

God was allowing circumstances to occur for their good but Naomi could only see emptiness as she was faced with yet another problem, their immediate need for food. What could she do? It seemed there was nothing she could do!

Reflecting on my situation after Alan's death, I can see many similarities. Fourteen weeks before Alan died he left his job where he had been employed for twenty- three years. He was obeying God's clear guidance to enter into a fulltime teaching ministry. This meant we were receiving no wages and it was a further two months after his death before I received any social welfare provision. Like Naomi, I had a home but no immediate source of income or food, yet unlike Naomi I also had three children to feed. What could I do? There was nothing immediate that I could do!

It is not God's desire for us to suffer one moment longer than we can bear, yet the Lord often has to bring us to a point where we can do absolutely nothing. It is then, in our emptiness, when we humbly bow before Him with "a broken and contrite heart" (Ps 51:17), that He does more than we can ask or think! He keeps His promise to "deliver the needy who cry out, the afflicted who have no one to help" (Psalm 72:12).

I have great delight in testifying that God provided far beyond our needs during those first two months and has continued to do so for the past seven years, in many and varied ways. This has been a humbling yet fulfilling experience. As I have drawn closer to God in my need, He has drawn closer to me.

> "But as for me, it is good to be near God. I have made the Sovereign Lord my refuge; I will tell of all your deeds"
>
> Psalm 73:28

Following God's ways

Ruth had remained silent at the city gate when confronted by Naomi's friends. She listened with empathy to Naomi's bitter lament but Ruth knew her mother-in-law had a strong faith in the God of Israel. During happier days in Moab she had grown to love and respect Naomi and her God. For this reason, when humanly speaking all seemed lost, Ruth was able to make a firm decision to follow Naomi.

As soon as they had reached the old homestead Ruth made another decision. She didn't sit and wait for some-thing to happen but took up the role of protector for her old and weary mother-in-law. Using her initiative she asked Naomi's permission to gather grain in the fields.

Naomi decided to stay home and allow her young daughter-in-law to go and gather food. This is perhaps best understood when we consider Dr Turnbull's observation that during this stage of depression and apathy the bereaved often withdraw from contact with people who will make demands upon them: 'They tend instead to rely on close friends *whom they expect to act as protectors*'.[16] As well as suffering this emotional stress, Naomi would have been physically exhausted by the long journey and glad to rest at home. They had walked through the barren desert around the Dead Sea and then over the hills and valleys of Israel before reaching Bethlehem.

While in Moab, Naomi must have taught Ruth about the laws of Moses because she acted on the law which commanded the reapers not to reap the edge of the fields but to leave it for the foreigner, fatherless and widow. When Ruth decided to go to the harvest fields she took a step of faith. She believed God would provide food for them in accordance with His laws.

Ruth was unaware at this stage of God's involvement, yet He was directing her steps. It was no accident that she found herself working in the field belonging to Boaz. God was accomplishing His purposes through Ruth but she was the one making the decisions. She acted in accordance with God's revealed will.

> ". . . love and faithfulness go before you. Blessed are those who have learned to acclaim you, who walk in the light of your presence, O Lord"
>
> Psalm 89:14,15

Ruth was not presumptuous, demanding that God's laws be obeyed. She humbly asked the foreman's permission to gather grain among the sheaves. With her request granted, she worked diligently, resting only when necessary. Suddenly her work was interrupted by the arrival of the owner of the field. He called out,"The Lord be with you!" and all the workers called back,"The Lord bless you!" She had never heard this greeting in Moab! Imagine her further surprise when Boaz singled her out and wanted to speak to her.

At this time there were many unscrupulous land- owners who took advantage of the poor and widowed, but Boaz is a remarkable example of a man who reflected the character of a loving God. This can be seen in his customary greeting to his workers and his compassion and generosity in obeying God's laws to provide for the poor, oppressed and widow. His genuine concern that a Moabite widow be cared for exceeded the law. His care for Ruth is seen in a progression of acts of kindness.

Firstly he called Ruth,"My daughter". This shows the integrity and tenderness of Boaz, as this term was how a father would address his daughter. Boaz then instructed Ruth not to glean anywhere but in his field and to stay with his servant girls.

Boaz wanted Ruth to receive a good return for her labour. He was also concerned for her protection. He told her to stay with his servant girls and instructed the men not "to touch" her. The word "touch" could mean 'beat violently', 'inflict injury' or 'have sexual relations', therefore Boaz was obviously sensitive to Ruth's vulnerability as a young unprotected widow.

The drink of water Boaz provided for Ruth while she worked in the scorching heat of the day, was an extraordinary favour. It was usually the responsibility of women to draw water for the men and it was customary for a foreigner to draw water for an Israelite.

His generosity and kindness overwhelmed Ruth. In humble gratitude she bowed down with her face to the ground and exclaimed, "Why have I found such favor in your eyes that you notice me–a foreigner?"

Boaz's reply makes it clear that he had already heard about Ruth's kindness toward Naomi. He knew she had left her parents, her homeland and her people and chosen to follow the God of Israel. He appreciated and honoured her for her integrity and faithfulness. It appears God had already inclined Boaz's heart towards Ruth.

Boaz prayed that the Lord would richly bless Ruth for what she had done. Although Boaz was looking after Ruth he acknowledged that it was actually God, under whose "wings" she had come "for refuge", who would reward her.

We must lay hold of this promise too. If we follow God's ways, finding our refuge in Him, He promises to guide and protect us in order to fulfil His good purposes for us.

> "I will take refuge in the shadow of your 'wings' until the disaster has passed. I cry out to God Most High, to God, who fulfills his purpose for me"
>
> Psalm 57:1,2

At mealtime Boaz said to her, "Come over here. Have some bread and dip it in the wine vinegar."

When she sat down with the harvesters, he offered her some roasted grain. She ate all she wanted and had some left over. As she got up to glean, Boaz gave orders to his men, "Even if she gathers among the sheaves, don't embarrass her. Rather, pull out some stalks for her from the bundles and leave them for her to pick up, and don't rebuke her".

So Ruth gleaned in the field until evening. Then she threshed the barley she had gathered, and it amounted to about an ephah. She carried it back to town, and her mother-in-law saw how much she had gathered. Ruth also brought out and gave her what she had left over after she had eaten enough.

Her mother-in-law asked her, "Where did you glean today? Where did you work? Blessed be the man who took notice of you!"

Then Ruth told her mother-in-law about the one at whose place she had been working. "The name of the man I worked with today is Boaz", she said.

"The Lord bless him!" Naomi said to her daughter-in-law. "He has not stopped showing his kindness to the Living and the dead." She added, "That man is our close relative; he is one of our kinsman-redeemers." Then Ruth the Moabitess said, "He even said to me, 'Stay with my workers until they finish harvesting all my grain'".

Naomi said to Ruth her daughter-in-law, "It will be good for you, my daughter, to go with his girls, because in someone else's field you might be harmed."

So Ruth stayed close to the servant girls of Boaz to glean until the barley and wheat harvests were finished. And she lived with her mother-in-law.

Ruth 2:14-23

Chapter 6

God Provides

As Ruth's first day in the gleaning field progressed, so did Boaz's generosity. He included Ruth at his meal table and served her himself. This was an act of extraordinary kindness which showed his workers that he accepted this Moabite widow as one with them. Ruth was given such a generous serving that she had enough to take home to share with Naomi. Boaz then ordered his men to allow Ruth to glean "among" the sheaves rather than just on the edge of the fields. They were told not to embarrass or rebuke her for doing so. As if that was not enough, he then exceeded all requirements of the law and told his men to purposely drop some grain for Ruth to pick up. Boaz's generosity was overwhelming.

God blesses those who obey

I believe Ruth was blessed because she had firstly given herself totally to God. When she left Moab as a poor destitute widow, she owned nothing and appears to have had no money or possessions to give, but she willingly gave herself. Paul reminds us in Romans 12:1,2 that God's will is that we offer our bodies as living sacrifices to Him. This means whatever our status–whether widowed, single, married or divorced–God wants us to give ourselves to Him.

While talking to a group of widows recently I was moved with compassion. One sat in a wheelchair suffering from multiple sclerosis. She related how her husband, just before he died, had wanted to leave her because of her illness. Another also sat in a wheelchair as she was blind and a diabetic. She related some incidents in her past life where she felt she had failed in her witness for God. She could see no good in herself, she felt she had nothing to give. All seemed hopeless.

I was humbled into silence for a few minutes while I inwardly thanked God that I had eyes that could see and legs that could walk, yet I saw in this weary and burdened widow something that God desired. He wanted her, with her disabilities and in her weakness, to come and give Him what she did have: herself. I shared this with her, assuring her that as she acted in obedience, God would bless her and transform her into a woman of influence for Him.God desires to work through us for His glory no matter what our status, disability or suffering. He is in the business of turning tragedies into triumph.

I had always understood that the offering of my body as a "living sacrifice" to God, meant a continual process of giving of myself. However, I had thought of my widowhood as a separate issue: a condition to be endured until God saw fit to provide another husband. It has been a struggle for me to let go of this concept and humbly surrender myself to God, as I am.I want to testify that this same God who blessed Ruth so many years ago, delights in pouring out His blessings today on those who surrender in obedience to Him, trusting that He will work through them.

Let me illustrate by sharing with you excerpts from one month of my diary. It reads very similarly to the account of the continued blessings that were poured upon Ruth. For me, like Ruth, it began with a step of faith in obedience to God's will.

God had been impressing upon me an urgency to finish writing this book. To be obedient however, meant dedicating my time fully to the task. It was necessary therefore, to leave my part-time secretarial job. This was a step in faith because I knew I would have to trust God to supply the extra money needed to supplement my fairly meagre widow's benefit.

Within weeks of having given my resignation I experienced an almost overwhelming number of financial problems. This caused me to question God. "Why are you allowing these problems to happen? Aren't I seeking to do what you have asked me to do?"

I could not understand. I did not know at the time, that God was allowing these difficulties to occur so that He could show me, in a special way, how much He loved and cared for me. The experiences that followed strengthened my faith. They acted as confirmation that God was pleased with my obedience and that I was doing His will. I will relate the problems as they occurred and then explain how God dealt with them, one at a time...

My house developed a leak which extended the entire length of the lower centre roof. When it rained the plastic one litre cartons I had placed along the centre beam, filled with water. I had previously been warned by a builder that because of an oversight by the original builders, the galvanised iron had rusted along the centre seam and would only last a few more years. It looked as if the few years were up. To replace the galvanised iron roof would cost thousands of dollars. The same week I was dismayed to see the floor of the shower-box collapse! The builder quoted over a thousand dollars to fix it because in order to replace the rotten floorboards underneath the shower, the whole showerbox needed to be removed and renewed!

During the same week, I had my car checked before going on our Christmas holiday. The mechanic informed me that although the oil leak in the car was not dangerous and I could keep using it, there was major work to be done which would cost $2000! As if that was not enough, my dishwasher stopped working. One side of the grill on my electric stove died and the cat got run over by a car and needed surgery on his mangled paw.

This didn't stop us from going away and enjoying our holiday. We returned two weeks later to all the problems. As planned, I left work but nothing was fixed and I had no money to pay for any repairs. The step in faith I had originally envisaged seemed to have become a giant leap. Convinced I was obeying the Lord, I committed the problems to Him and started writing.

The Christian builder who provided a quote to fix the showerbox had a look at the roof and to my surprise, could find no rust! The original builder who had said it was rusty and would need replacing in a few years was also a Christian. Did the Lord remove the rust? I don't know, but it was able to be resealed for $50 and has shown no signs of leaking since!

We used the showerbox with the floor temporarily propped up by a piece of wood while I endeavoured to claim insurance to cover the cost of repairs. My efforts were unsuccessful and the wood prop began to give way. During the next week a friend who wondered why I hadn't got the showerbox repaired offered to pay the bill. Not only did my friend show kindness but so did the Christian builder. He sent me a second quote deducting his labour charges! This man did not know my financial position but was simply prompted by the Lord. The showerbox was fixed the next week. Praise God!

I thought to myself, "I guess the car is next." When visiting some friends a few weeks later they handed me an envelope saying they had felt prompted by the Lord to give me some money. The envelope contained $1000. "Wow!" I thought, "this must be to fix my car." I had the car re-checked and the oil leak only cost $200. The balance covered the out-standing bills which had accumulated over the Christmas break.

Not only did God display His love and kindness by supplying all our needs but He went further. He gave a further gift specifically designated for me to spend on myself!

All this happened within the first month of leaving work. I felt humbled yet elated–just as Ruth must have felt when returning home to Naomi at the end of her first day in the fields! Her pockets bulged with the left-over food from lunch and she carried an amazingly large quantity of barley. (An ephah was equivalent to at least half a month's wages.[17])

I can imagine Naomi anxiously waiting at home for Ruth's return from the fields. She may have spent the day resting after the long and dangerous walk from Moab or she could have spent the day cleaning-up the old derelict home. We are not told. Naomi was overcome with the quantity of grain Ruth brought home. "Where did you glean today? Where did you work?" she asked excitedly. Not waiting for a reply she exclaimed, *"Blessed be the man who took notice of you!"*

God blesses through others

Sometimes I wonder if today it has become a duty rather than an act of love and kindness to care for the bereaved. Modern Western society lives for the enjoy-ment of today with very little thought about death. Is it because the widow is a reminder of death that she is often left alone? Is she compelled in our society to hide her grief in order to gain acceptance? Sadly this seems to be the case, even in the church. Many Christians have the warped view that Christians should not weep or show grief. In their opinion, it seems the bereaved should remain firm and unmoved–indicating a deep spiritual faith!

An incident I read recently illustrates this view. A pastor conducting a seminar on 'Understanding Grief' was interrupted by a widow who timidly said, "One of my sisters scolded me for weeping once. She said I didn't show much faith, that I wasn't acting like a Christian."

The Pastor sighed and said he had heard similar comments too often before. He went on to encourage her by saying that sorrow did not indicate lack of faith, for even Christ sought refuge with His closest friends in His time of sorrow. 'How much more this well meaning sister would have helped if she'd just held Jan's hand and said, "*Do weep, I understand*,"'[18]

Care for orphans and widows was commanded in the Old Testament as a way of imitating God's character. So too the early Christians were reminded that acts of love and kindness towards orphans and widows pleased God the Father. James 1:27 says, "Religion that God our Father accepts as pure and faultless is this: to look after orphans and widows in their distress. . . "

James uses the Greek word 'episkeptesthai', translated "to look after." This can also be translated "to visit"(KJV). It has a 'present continuous sense,'[19] indicating the need for continuous help for the widow and orphan. It is the same word the people used when describing Jesus' action after the resurrection of the widow of Nain's son: "God has come 'to help' his people" (Lk 7:16). It is the same word used by the Lord when He spoke of how He would recognise His followers on the day of judgment: "I needed clothes and you clothed me, I was sick and you 'looked after' me" (Matt 25:36).

James uses the Greek word 'thlipsis', translated "distress" which primarily means 'a pressure; anything which burdens the spirit.'[20] Distress for the widow could mean anything, from the deep suffering of grief, to lack of physical strength needed in practical daily living or the need for financial assistance.

It is not just a social call that James is talking about. It is continuous action from a heart of love to care for those in need. It may be as simple as sitting and listening to a widow pour out her feelings of grief. It may be splitting of logs for her winter fire or simply fixing a dripping tap. Whatever it is, it is the way God's people today are to act. It is action which reflects to others the character of God.

Unfortunately this art of shared grief is not always experienced because of our Anglo-Saxon heritage of the 'stiff upper lip'. Remember, Jesus wept because He was "deeply moved in spirit" when He saw Mary and the Jews weeping for His friend Lazarus who had died (Jn 11:33). We need to learn from Him. He is the God of all comfort, who shares in our grief. We will then be able to come alongside the bereaved and share in their grief.

Once Naomi learned that the man who had helped Ruth was Boaz she immediately prayed for the Lord's blessing on him. She recognised him as a close relative, one who could act as their 'kinsman-redeemer'. When she mentioned this to Ruth it didn't seem to mean too much to her, for she continued on with her conversation about Boaz. It appears that Ruth did not, at this stage, understand the significance of a kinsman -redeemer's role in a 'levirate' marriage. This was a custom where the closest male relative of a man who had died, was expected to take his relative's widow as his wife. He was to raise up children to carry on the dead man's name and inherit his property.[21]

Naomi who understood the custom, was excited! Hope filled her heart as she recognised God's goodness expressed through the kindness of Boaz. She changed from being an inward-looking and depressed widow to mirror Ruth's upward and outward looking demeanour. She began to appreciate her daughter-in-law in a new way. God had not brought her back "empty" after all!

Naomi emerged from her cloud of depression with a renewed sense of God's love and care. She began to think of the future instead of dwelling on the past. In fact, a great plan formed in her mind! God however, had an even greater plan, a plan in which these two widows would become women of influence for Him.

The gold goes through the fire
To prove that it is real,
And when our faith is tested,
What will it then reveal?
For suffering brings us patience,
And patience when complete,
Will make our faith mature,
And keep us from defeat.

So even when we're suffering,
We know that God is near.
His arms are wrapped around us,
He sees each falling tear.
He knows about our anguish
For he has suffered too.
Rejoice in such a friend,
For he will see us through.

Excerpt from *Rejoice in the Lord Always* by
Kath Howan

One day Naomi her mother-in-law said to her, 'My daughter, should I not try to find a home for you, where you will be well provided for? Is not Boaz, with whose servant girls you have been, a servant of ours? Tonight he will be winnowing barley on the threshing floor. Wash and perfume yourself, and put on your best clothes. Then go down to the threshing floor, but don't let him know you are there until he has finished eating and drinking. When he lies down, note the place where he is lying. Then go and uncover his feet and lie down. He will tell you what to do.

'I will do whatever you say,' Ruth answered. So she went down to the threshing floor and did everything her mother-in-law told her to do.

Ruth 3:1-6

Chapter 7

Facing the Future

In the early stages of grief I remember feeling very much like Naomi must have felt as she lamented before her friends on her return to Bethlehem. Trying to come to terms with my pain I climbed a hill behind our home to be alone with God. When I reached the top of the hill, having wept all the way, I viewed the panorama of the valley floor stretching approximately thirty kilometres from the coastline to the mountain ranges. In the other direction was the harbour embracing the city of Wellington and beyond.

As I looked up the valley, I wept bitterly for I could see in the distance the graveyard where I knew Alan's body lay. I prayed that I would see some sanity in God's decision to take Alan to be with Himself.

Lifting my head, I was struck by the beauty and grandeur of the mountain ranges and the harbour. I marvelled at God's creation. I then looked at the tiny homes that specked the hillsides and valley floor and thought how insignificant man's little creations were in comparison to God's mighty creation which surrounded me. Filled with a fresh sense of God's creative power and goodness my heart was strengthened. I was reminded that this mighty God who created all things had everything under His control. He had not made a mistake. All was in His plan. I simply had to trust Him!

I turned from the view of the distant cemetery towards the city and prayed fervently that God would strengthen me to face the future and help me not to keep looking back at the past.

As I walked back down the hill a large bird flew past and spiralled high above. I watched until it disappeared into the blue expanse. The Holy Spirit impressed upon my mind the words of Isaiah. . .

> "Those who hope in the Lord will renew their strength. They will soar on wings like eagles; they will run and not grow weary, they will walk and not be faint"
>
> Isaiah 40:31

I returned home singing, with my strength renewed in the Lord, conscious that I had taken a major step forward in my grieving. I had gained a little more understanding of what the apostle Peter meant when he wrote: ". . . those who suffer according to God's will should commit themselves to their faithful Creator and continue to do good" (1 Peter 4:19).

God is the One who understands our heart and He is the One who wants to share in our grief. He is the One who gives joy amidst sorrow and He is the One who has promised never to leave us but to protect and provide for us. He simply waits to heal and make whole the broken and contrite heart of those who call on Him. He fills the empty heart with His love and compassion. His strength renews us so that we can walk again and not faint.

When Naomi returned to Bethlehem she was unable to see how this would happen but she trusted God to keep His promises to defend, love, feed and clothe the widow.[22] God rewarded her through the kindness of Ruth and Boaz.

Becoming whole again

Naomi came to a place of surrender to God when she agreed with Ruth's suggestion to obey God's law of gathering grain for their food. Through Ruth's acceptance and obedience to God's revealed will and Boaz's kindness, Naomi experienced God's blessing and was strengthened and encouraged in her faith. She saw herself again as a woman of worth.

Ruth loved her mother-in-law unconditionally. This was not because of anything she might gain but because she saw in her someone of worth, someone whose life she wanted to affirm.

This is the kind of love Jesus encouraged. The New Testament Christians used the Greek word 'agape' to express the same kind of love. Thomas Jones explains what happens when a person chooses to love with agape-love: '. . . he does not focus on what he is feeling or needing, nor does he focus on what he expects to gain by loving. Instead, he focuses on the good of the other person.' [23]

God wants us to love each other with agape-love. Paul says: "Do nothing out of selfish ambition or vain conceit, but in humility consider others better than yourselves" (Phil 2:3).

When love is given in this way to others, it has a boomerang effect. The giver is also blessed.

In response to Ruth's kindness, Naomi acts with the same kind of selfless love towards Ruth. Naomi had thought of herself as a widow of no importance, but now with renewed confidence she becomes instrumental in answering her own prayer. She had prayed that Ruth would find 'rest' in the home of another husband. Naomi herself, could have legitimately sought protection in a levirate marriage with Boaz but she was only interested in Ruth's welfare.

Naomi's prayer was completely unselfish. She was not thinking of herself but of Ruth's wellbeing as an unprotected widow in a foreign land. No mention is made of her land nor of an heir. Her main objective for Ruth's remarriage was that she might find companionship, protection and security.

It may seem to some that Naomi was being an interfering mother-in-law but in the ancient East it was customary and considered the responsibility of parents, to arrange marriages for their children. This is not as barbaric as it seems. Most marriages were between teenagers and matchmaking parents probably had a shrewder idea of compatibility than the adolescents[24]

This is still a custom in many parts of the world–China, India and Africa, to name a few. Lin Yu-tang, the Chinese writer and philosopher, believed the Western system was 'cruelty' compared to the Orient, where parents considered it their most important duty to find a suitable mate for their sons and daughters. He considered that because parents have a lifelong knowledge of their children they can judge far better, the most suitable temperament needed in a match, rather than leaving it to the child's chance, emotional 'falling in love'.[25]

To our Western minds this is a foreign custom and it seems a rather 'forward' step for Ruth to claim Boaz as a husband. However, because Ruth was accepted by God and His people, she was able to see herself as a person of worth again. She was able to accept her mother-in-law's advice and understood her action to be a step of obedience to God's levirate law.

When is a widow ready for remarriage?

Was Ruth ready for remarriage? Had she developed a new image of herself as a single person? A whole person? It is of utmost importance for a widow to have reached this stage of seeing herself as a whole person in Christ before entering into a second marriage. The feeling of being cut-in-half must change. A widow must be whole again to be able to give herself wholly to another.

Ruth trusted Naomi's wisdom and followed her instructions implicitly. She washed, anointed herself and changed her clothes. As previously pointed out, abstinence from personal anointing was often practised as a sign of mourning. The wearing of a widow's garment was also the usual procedure for widows of the ancient Middle East but Naomi wanted Ruth to change and appear as attractive as possible to take up the role of 'suitor'. For Ruth to agree to take off her widow's garments and anoint herself was, I believe, indicative of her emergence from the grieving process. She showed a readiness for remarriage.

Ruth's action reminds me of a similar action I took about two years after Alan's death. There is no custom in our country with regard to what a widow does or doesn't wear. I recall feeling confused and unsure whether I should keep wearing my wedding ring on my left hand when I was really no longer married.

All other widows I knew kept wearing their wedding rings on their left hand, but I felt I was not being honest about my situation. I struggled with this for about a year and was encouraged to read a comment by Nancy Johnson in her book *Alone and Beginning Again*. She said that one of the first 'breakthroughs' in her steps towards beginning again, was when she took her wedding and engagement rings from her left hand and put them on her right hand. It was only then that she saw herself as 'officially' single. [26]

When I decided to take this step I felt I was officially acknowledging to myself and to others that I was no longer married but single again. This was a definite step in my grieving process, but it did not mean that I was ready for remarriage. I had not at this stage "...learned to be content whatever the circumstances" (Phil 4:11). I had not learnt to look beyond my status and rest in Christ as His disciple.

When Ruth decided to follow God she put every thought of herself aside. She found contentment and satisfaction in helping her aged mother-in-law. She did not seek marriage as a way of escape from her widowhood. If this had been her aim she would not have chosen to follow Naomi to Bethlehem. Instead she would have returned to the land of Moab with Orpah, or married one of the young eligible men from among the reapers.

Unfortunately, remarriage is too often sought as an escape from the loneliness and frustration of widowhood. It is easy to rush into remarriage and accept the advances of any man instead of waiting on the Lord for His timing and His choice of partner.

I was warned of this earlier in my widowhood when I was being harrassed by several men who thought they would make suitable husbands for me! A friend, who was concerned about my vulnerability, related an incident which occurred some years ago. A widow had married a man who, while courting her, acted as a loving and caring Christian towards her and her three children. Desperately wanting to be remarried and for her children to have a loving father again, she believed his lies and married him. It was only a matter of months before she realised the mistake she had made. He had got what he wanted and took off, leaving her and her children homeless. She suffered many financial and emotional problems.

In her book, *After the Flowers Have Gone*, Bea Decker relates several sad cases of widows who rushed into second marriages only to live regretting their decisions. She sums up with two warnings: 'Never decide you need to remarry and grab for a partner' and 'be more cautious and take more time'. From her experience gained through many years of working with the widowed, she concludes: 'happy second marriages were almost directly in proportion to successful readjustment after losing one's first mate'. [27]

It is not wrong for a widow to desire to be remarried. Nor is it wrong for her to want to remain single. If a widow has experienced a happy marriage then it is a normal and healthy reaction to want to be in that same position of enjoyment again. Yet, for the very same reason, some find it hard to believe that they could experience such a good marriage again and dismiss the possibility of it ever occurring. There are still others, who having experienced an unhappy marriage, are glad of the freedom from that bond.

The widow will find that there are always those who freely give their advice regarding remarriage. One friend who encouraged remarriage commented, "to want to remarry is a compliment to your previous husband".

Is God my husband?

As well as those who encouraged remarriage, I had other well-meaning comforters pat me on the shoulder and say, “God is your husband now!” This did not comfort–it confused me. I felt as if a band-aid had been slapped across my gaping wound in the hope that it would heal!

Thinking I must be very unspiritual, I decided to examine the verse quoted from Isaiah.

It was a relief to me to discover that this bold statement in Isaiah 54:5 “..your Maker is your husband ,” was speaking metaphorically of the restoration of Israel after her exile.

In the Old Testament, the metaphor of the husband/wife relationship was often used to illustrate the closeness of the bond between God and the nation of Israel.[28] Just as in the New Testament the Church is referred to as the Bride of Christ.

Isaiah, in this passage, likens Israel’s time of separation in exile to widowhood. He stresses that the renewed relationship between God and Israel was like the close bond of a husband/wife relationship. To apply this statement to the widow today, is therefore taking it completely out of context and applying a wrong meaning to the text.

God does not literally, nor in some mystical sense, become a husband to the widow, just as He does not become a wife for the widower! Whether one is single, married, divorced or widowed, we all have a unique relationship with God.

In one sense only can this be likened to a husband/wife relationship. Our lives have been joined as one with God and as we become more closely drawn to Him in love, our two wills become one, with one purpose.

Successful readjustment

It is important to take heed of Bea Decker's advice. There must be successful readjustment after losing our first husband before considering remarriage. We have to allow time for the completion of the grieving process and time to readjust to 'singleness'. It may take months or years to find our true identity in Christ and to live a happy and fulfilled 'single' life as His disciple. We need to realise that as His disciple He has a plan and purpose for us in our time of singleness.

After Ruth made the decision to commit herself totally to God and follow His ways, she experienced God's compassion through the kindness and generosity of Boaz. He accepted her and treated her with overwhelming kindness because he saw her as a woman of integrity. She was obviously content in her life with Naomi. Had Ruth successfully readjusted to her singleness? Was she ready for remarriage?

When Naomi suggested to Ruth that she should ask Boaz to fulfil the levirate law, she did not blindly obey Naomi's instructions. During the six to eight weeks of harvesting, Ruth talked and ate with Boaz and mutual respect had developed. Ruth knew from her first introduction to Boaz that he was a man of God. Through his words and actions she experienced kindness, compassion and generosity. Because Ruth had confidence in his integrity she didn't hesitate to obey Naomi. She took the step and claimed his protection in marriage.

For Boaz, it had been Ruth's noble character that first attracted him. He had heard of her kindness to Naomi before he had even met her. It was her noble character that Boaz valued when faced with the decision regarding marriage. It was not Ruth's status, role, beauty or talents that attracted Boaz. It was her character he valued and it was her character that gained her praise from the townsfolk. As Watson says: *'The truth was that she had met with a man of character who valued character'.*[29]

Ruth could have looked inwardly and seen herself as a poor foreign widow who owned nothing, and who carried the extra burden of caring for an old mother-in-law. Instead Ruth's attitude and actions of love, despite her difficult circumstances, revealed her noble character. With her relationship with God in correct focus she was happy and fulfilled in following His ways and serving others. She was whole again! She was ready for remarriage!

When we humbly bow before God, offering ourselves as a living sacrifice we regain a sense of self-worth. We realise anew that our true identity lies in Christ as His disciple, no matter what our status–widowed, single, married, or whatever–we accept that God sees us as worthy, not because of what we are or anything we may have done but because He is the One who values us. He values us so highly that He sent His son to die for us! "This is how we know what love is: Jesus Christ laid down his life for us. And we ought to lay down our lives for our brothers"... "We love because He first loved us" (1 John 3:16; 4:19).

Before I can consider remarriage I must ask myself, "Am I ready for remarriage? Am I seeing myself as a whole person again in Christ? Am I following and obeying Christ's commands as His disciple, loving others unconditionally as Ruth and Naomi were?" In loving this way, a widow becomes whole and will be able to give herself wholly to another.

If she is not whole then she cannot be a true "help meet" for a new husband (Gen 2:18 KJV). A "help meet" means a helper suitable as a counterpart: a companion who is able to share joys, sorrows, fears, problems and to work with side by side. To be able to "desire the highest good in the one loved, even to the point of self-sacrifice"[30] is essential.

Perhaps the hardest thing of all
That we on earth must face,
Is when we find the ones we love
Are taken from their place.
They walked along life's road with us
Brought comfort, joy and love,
And then their work on earth complete
God called them home above.
It feels as if your heart will break,
so great your grief and pain -
You wonder if you'll ever feel
As if you're whole again:
But, think a moment in this time
When many tears may fall;
God brings a word of hope to one
Who knows that God is all.
'Come close my child,' He gently says,
'You have in Me a friend,
You know I'll never let you go
I'll keep you 'til life's end.
Remember that I died for you,
Through death I gave you life,
You learn to love me less through ease
Than you will learn through strife.'
Through suffering you will find with time
Though now it's hard to see;
You'll help one day another bear
Their own sad tragedy.[31]

When Boaz had finished eating and drinking and was in good spirits, he went over to lie down at the far end of the grain pile. Ruth approached quietly, uncovered his feet and lay down. In the middle of the night something startled the man, and he turned and discovered a woman lying at his feet.

"Who are you?" he asked.

"I am your servant Ruth," she said. "Spread the corner of your garment over me, since you are a kinsman-redeemer,"

"The Lord bless you, my daughter," he replied. "This kindness is greater than that which you showed earlier: You have not run after the younger men, whether rich or poor.

And now, my daughter, don't be afraid. I will do for you all you ask. All my fellow townsmen know that you are a woman of noble character. Although it is true that I am near of kin, there is a kinsman-redeemer nearer than I. Stay here for the night, and in the morning if he wants to redeem, good; let him redeem. But if he is not willing, as surely as the Lord lives I will do it. Lie here until morning."

So she lay at his feet until morning, but got up before anyone could be recognised; and he said, "Don't let it be known that a woman came to the threshing floor."

He also said, "Bring me the shawl you are wearing and hold it out." When she did so, he poured into it six measures of barley and put it on her. Then he went back to town.

Ruth 3:7-15

Chapter 8

Should I Remarry?

There will always be widows who desire remarriage and there will be those who have no desire to remarry. Ruth and Naomi were both prepared and able to give themselves wholly to another in marriage. Naomi however put this thought aside, yet sought remarriage for her daughter-in-law and Ruth happily agreed with the suggestion.

For many who lose their husband in later life, the question of remarriage isn't even considered. Some widows who have enjoyed a happy marriage, believe it impossible to expect to find such happiness again. Others who have a strong desire to remarry, believe God is quite capable of richly blessing another marriage.

Widows who have been left with children to bring up often see remarriage as adding another difficulty to their already emotionally stretched lives. There are many others however, who would happily embrace the love and wise counsel of another husband to help with the rearing of their children.

I have listened to many reasons why widows wish to stay single. One very misguided reasoning is from those who believe that to marry another man is displaying an unfaithful love to their former husband. This not only over-rides the marriage vow: " 'til death do us part," but is infinitely more pious than the Biblical requirement.

What does God say about remarriage?

The apostle Paul states in Romans 7:2-3: ". . . by law a married woman is bound to her husband as long as he is alive, but if her husband dies, she is released from the law of marriage. . . and is not an adulteress, even though she marries another man." Again in 1 Corinthians 7:39 he states: "A woman is bound to her husband as long as he lives. But if her husband dies, she is free to marry anyone she wishes, but he must belong to the Lord."

• A new covenant

When I studied the verses in Romans 7, I was reminded of the permanency of the marriage covenant. It is a covenant that God views as ending only with death.

Paul was teaching the Christians in Rome that they were no longer under the old covenant of law but under the new covenant of grace. He taught that it was only death–the death of Christ–that released believers from the old covenant so "that they might belong to another." To illustrate this important truth he used the example of a widow who remarries as coming under a new covenant.

When marriage takes place, the vow "'til death do us part" is a covenant made between husband, wife and God. When death occurs that covenant has ended. Jesus said in Matthew 5:17 that He had not come to "abolish" the old covenant but to "fulfill" it. The widow should not see her marriage vow as abolished or broken, but fulfilled. *It is complete!* It is only divorce that is spoken of as a "broken" covenant.

When Jesus was questioned by the Pharisees about divorce, He reminded them that when a man is united to his wife and becomes one flesh, it is God who joins them together and nobody should separate them (Matt 19:6). He said this at a time when Jewish law did not allow a wife the right of divorce, yet allowed a husband to divorce his wife for the most minor offences. The rabbis had distorted the law of Moses to the extent that a husband could divorce his wife if she spoiled his food, or if she went out with her hair unbound, or decided to spin in the street or speak with any other man.[32]

Jesus corrected this distorted view of treating a wife as a mere chattel that could be so easily discarded. He made one exception to the permanency of the marriage covenant. Jesus graciously permitted divorce if there existed any marital unfaithfulness. However, this was seen by God as a "broken" covenant: ". . . the Lord is acting as the witness between you and the wife of your youth, because you have broken faith with her, though she is your partner, the wife of your marriage covenant" (Mal 2:14).

The old covenant of Law served the purposes for which it had been given and with Christ's death it became a 'completed' covenant.

When death occurs, it is important to remember this is God's prerogative. When a Christian dies then that person has completed God's purpose for which he or she was born. Just as David "...served God's purpose in his own generation... and... fell asleep" (Acts 13:36).

When we grasp this truth and realise that our first marriage is a completed and fulfilled covenant, then we will be able to view remarriage positively. It would be a new covenant for which God has a plan and purpose.

• Sexually and socially vulnerable

Looking again at the story of Ruth, we see in this climactic scene of the threshing floor, the secret meeting between Ruth and Boaz. The reason for the secrecy was, I believe, for Ruth's physical protection and the protection of her reputation.

It was the possibility of Ruth's visit being misinterpreted that concerned Naomi. She knew the usual festivity and the accompanying licentious behaviour associated with the threshing floor (Hosea 9:1). That is why she told Ruth to note the location where Boaz slept and approach him when it was dark so she would not be recognised by the workers.

Boaz also understood the vulnerable position that Ruth had put herself in by coming to the threshing floor. This is why he advised her to stay with him for the remainder of the night and leave in the morning before she could be recognised. Not only could their meeting be misinterpreted by others around (and interestingly is still being misinterpreted by commentators today), but there would be every possibility of her being physically abused by workers who had joined in the festivities.

Ruth had been in a vulnerable situation when working in the harvest fields but at the threshing floor where prostitution was openly practised, she was in an extremely precarious position. Naomi, fully aware of the immoral activities that took place at these festivities, obviously trusted Ruth and Boaz to act with integrity and personal restraint.

Many years later, the Apostle Paul was deeply concerned with the vulnerability of widows in the early church. This prompted him to write to the church at Corinth with instructions for their protection. There were even more comprehensive instructions in his letter to Timothy!

Many have accused Paul of having a low view of women and marriage. However, a careful study of these passages reveals that Paul, like Jesus, was in the business of uplifting womanhood in a society where women were considered inferior and where widows were often neglected or exploited.

• 1 Timothy 5:3-16

"Give proper recognition to those widows who are really in need. . . .No widow may be put on the list of widows unless she is over sixty, has been faithful to her husband, and is well known for her good deeds. . . .As for younger widows, do not put them on such a list. For when their sensual desires overcome their dedication to Christ, they want to marry. . . .So I counsel younger widows to marry, to have children, to manage their homes and to give the enemy no opportunity for slander" (v3,9,11,14)

When Paul wrote this letter to Timothy he was reminding the church to honour widows. He told them to consider the good deeds of widows and the important role they play in the church. This was in sharp contrast to the teaching of the rabbis who thought of women as having 'no wisdom except with the distaff (spindle).' [33] They considered women to be incapable of comprehending the law therefore, they were not permitted to attend rabbinical schools. It was an era when women were considered so inferior that Rabbi Judah ben Elai made the offensive statement:

> 'A man is bound to say the following three blessings daily: "Blessed art thou. . . who hast not made me a heathen. . . who hast not made me a woman. . . and who hast not made me a brutish man"'.[34]

Paul wrote to Christians in the early church and in a different culture, but we cannot dismiss the instructions as having no relevance for the widow today.

The sexual and social vulnerability of today's widow remains just as poignant in the early church era. How then should a widow in today's world react to Paul's advice?

When Paul wrote this letter he was conscious of the marriage laws of the Greeks, Romans and Jews who made provision for their widows. He was exasperated by the selfishness of some families in the Ephesian church because their ethics had fallen below those of the surrounding unbelievers. Some widows had relatives who could have financially supported them but were neglecting this responsibility. This neglect by relatives was causing problems of administration in the church. Their resources were being so stretched they were unable to adequately meet the needs of the widows without families.

Although Paul recognised the need for the church to support all widows who didn't have relatives who could help, he did not want younger widows to be placed on the "list" for *permanent* support.

The stipulation that a widow must be over sixty to be on the permanent support list, reflects the cultural thought-pattern of the Jews. They believed that old age began with the sixtieth year. The Romans also equated sixty years with the loss of physical powers and the diminishing of sexual passion.

Paul describes the younger widow as having "sensual desires". This literally means 'to feel the impulse of sexual desire'. Because her sexual passion is still a potent factor in her make-up, he is anxious that she is not subjected to a"pledge" of dedication that would be very difficult to keep. This appears to be the principal reason for not enrolling the younger widow. It indicates that a decision of celibacy was implicit when a widow enrolled for permanent support from the church. Ralph Earle likens this restraint placed on a young widow, to be like that 'of a young animal trying to free itself from the yoke, and becoming restive through its fulness of life'. [35]

Previous experience of *younger widows on the permanent support list* had resulted in many problems. Some had abandoned the path of self-denial and fallen into some form of indiscretion or immorality due to their sexual vulnerability. Others, due to their social vulnerability got into the habit of going from house to house filling their time with foolish gossip. They were prying into the private affairs of others and saying things they shouldn't. This had ruined their testimony and brought disgrace to the church.

Paul's advice to the "younger widow" is not to place herself under a permanent bond of celibacy but to remarry.

In his letter to the Corinthian church Paul shows the same understanding and concern for the social and sexual vulnerability of the widow.

• 1 Corinthians 7:1-40

"Now to the unmarried and the widows I say: It is good for them to stay unmarried, as I am. But if they cannot control themselves, they should marry, for it is better to marry than to burn with passion. . . A woman is bound to her husband as long as he lives. But if her husband dies, she is free to marry anyone she wishes, but he must belong to the Lord. In my judgment, she is happier if she stays as she is" (v8,9,39,40)

It is important to remember that when Paul wrote these words he was addressing a particular situation. The Christians in Corinth had become entangled with the ascetic lifestyle, to the extent that they believed sexual intercourse was intrinsically wrong. This had resulted in the belief that those who were married should abstain from intercourse (v2-7). They also thought Christians should divorce in order to avoid defilement by intercourse (v10-16), and remarriage of the widow was not approved (v8-9).

Paul was keen to see men and women live a celibate life in "undivided devotion to the Lord" (v35) but he recognised that celibacy was a "gift" from God and only given to some (v7). He taught, as did Jesus, that a celibate lifestyle was only to be chosen for the specific purpose of furthering the kingdom of God (Matt 19:10-12). He advised those who were married to continue in their marriages and the single or widowed were encouraged to consider continuing in the single life, but not required to seek it. Neither course was to be viewed as wrong or sinful.[36]

Paul was concerned that no man or woman should attempt a way of life for which they were naturally unfitted. Nobody should set out on a pathway where they deliberately surround themselves with temptations.

His advice to the unmarried and widow was: "It is good for them to stay unmarried, as I am" (that is, if they have the gift of celibacy). However, if they could not control themselves Paul advised them to remarry: "For it is better to marry than to burn with passion" (v9).

Dorothy Pape comments on this verse:

> 'Contrary to what has often been taught in the past this 'burning' is not of itself immoral but is only the intense desire for the fulfillment of a God-given instinct of the human body. In some people it appears to be stronger than in others'[37]

This is *revolutionary* teaching! In an era when women were mainly thought of as mere chattels and divorced for minor offences, Paul recognised that women as well as men, have a strong sexual drive. He also taught that women, as well as men, have the need and right to have that desire met: ". . . each man should have his own wife, and each woman her own husband" (v2).

Again, Paul announced a freedom which would not have existed under the customary arranged marriages of the East. He stated that a widow could marry anyone she wished (v39). This would also have freed her from any obligation to fulfil the 'levirate' law. The only stipulation was, if she remarried she must marry a believer.

When Paul wrote to the Christians at Thessalonica he gave the following instructions on "how to live in order to please God":

> "It is God's will that you should be sanctified: that you should avoid sexual immorality; that each of you should learn to control his own body (or lit. 'learn to live with his own wife'; or 'learn to acquire a wife' NIV note) in a way that is holy and honorable"
>
> 1 Thess 4:3

For the Christian, it is God's will that sexual union belong exclusively within the framework of marriage. As we have already noted, a freedom was given to the woman as well as the man, to choose whether or not to remarry. Remarriage therefore, is a matter of choice. For the widow it will depend on how strong her desire to remarry is. More importantly, it will depend upon God's future plan and purpose for her life! As she desires to live to please God and walk in step with the Spirit, He will guide and direct in the right pathway.

Paul made another revolutionary statement regarding freedom when he said that a widow would be happy if she remained unmarried (v40). This was a surprising claim in a society which for centuries had believed marriage and children were a sign of God's blessing, but widowhood and barrenness were a 'reproach' indicating God's displeasure. However, this statement has to be viewed in the light of two facts.

First, Paul believed "the time was short"(v29) before the return of Christ and secondly, because of "the present crisis"(v26) that existed at the time of writing this letter to the Corinthians.*

In both letters Paul recommends that younger widows should remarry. This reflects Paul's overall understanding of their sexual and social vulnerability, in a society where there existed little prospect of employment apart from prostitution. In those days the city of Corinth was well known for its temple of Aphrodite which, at one time, had in service one thousand prostitute priestesses[38]

There is a vast difference in our Western culture today. Relatives are under no legal responsibility to support a member of the family who may become widowed, and there are many job opportunities for the younger widow. Some receive income from insurance or business shares and in many countries, the government provides a benefit. To a large extent, this has lifted the financial responsibility for the care of the widow from the shoulders of the church or relatives. However, in countries where there exists no financial support from the government, the teachings

† The present crisis of v26 has been seen to be:
- A severe famine and the accompanying social dislocation of disorder and riots (B.Winter 'Tyndale Bulletin' 40, 1989) pp86-106.
- Persecution... arrests, beatings, imprisonment and killings because of the preaching of the gospel.
- Paul may have sensed the coming Roman persecutions, the first of which began under Nero some ten years after Paul wrote 1 Corinthians (J.McArthur Jnr, 1 Corinthians, Moody 1984) p179.

of Paul must be taken seriously and where appropriate, acted on.

Paul was not just concerned with the vulnerability of the widow in a society which may have neglected or exploited her, he was every bit as concerned with her personal and sexual vulnerability.

My vulnerability

If we're honest, most of us will admit that we struggle with our own sexual vulnerability in the same way as the widows in Paul's day. It would be most unnatural for one who has enjoyed the full expression of sexual intimacy in marriage not to miss that, when the death of a spouse occurs. Satan is fully aware of this. He is just as active today in seeking to attack us at our weakest point as he was in the early church era.

Satan, knowing my own sexual vulnerability, has tempted me a number of times on this issue. Earlier in my widowhood, when the numbness that accompanies grief had faded away and I was raw with loneliness and lack of intimacy, Satan began tempting me. It was at a time when I was surrounded by people who were openly enjoying sexual immorality.

On one occasion on my way home from visiting a sick relative and having an hour to spare, I decided to visit a friend. As I walked up to her home I picked up a crumpled piece of magazine on her pathway, intending to put it into her rubbish bin. I was somewhat shocked to discover it was a glossy page out of a pornographic magazine with photographs of explicit sexual acts. My initial reaction was to throw it away but as my friend was not home, and realising the possibility of her children seeing it on their way home from school, I took it home to destroy it.

Not wanting to risk the possibility of my own children finding it in the rubbish bin, I decided to burn it. I used a complete box of matches but the glossy page wouldn't burn. Being unsuccessful, I lit a fire in the wood-burner and it was only then that the page actually burned.

As I watched to make sure it was totally burnt, I noticed the colours fade into a negative and the words of Paul came graphically before me: "the widow who lives for pleasure is dead even while she lives" (1 Tim 5:6). Although the woman in the photograph was no doubt still living, she was dead in her sins.

A few days later, I parked the car at a lookout point to enjoy the scenic view of Wellington harbour. My son, who at eight years old was not too interested in the view, found a packet of photographs lying in the grass. After looking at some of them he handed them to me saying, "Mum, these are rude!" They were indeed, for what he showed me was a series of photographs taken of a male stripper at a nightclub.

Satan failed. He had overstepped himself, as he often does in his attacks. Instead of inciting me to follow the path of immorality I was sickened by the depravity of these men and women who openly displayed sex as a mere physical act to give erotic pleasure. I was annoyed that my son had been subjected to the sight of such sexually explicit photos. I prayed earnestly that the Lord would protect me from any more of Satan's attempts to test my vulnerability. I put my hope in God, continuing "night and day to pray and to ask God for help" (1 Tim 5:5).

God's protection

Returning to the scene at the threshing floor we witness a proposal of marriage. Ruth, who had found Boaz sleeping at the far end of the grain pile, waited until it was dark. She then uncovered his feet and lay down. After a short time Boaz awoke, probably with cold feet! He asked, "Who are you?" Ruth's reply was a customary proposal of marriage: "Spread the corner of your garment over me, since you are a kinsman-redeemer".

According to custom, marriages were solemnized among the Jews when the man threw the skirt of his talith or robe over his wife and covered her head with it.[39] The Arabs of early days also spread their skirt over a widow as a way of claiming her as their wife. Apparently this custom still exists among some modern Arabs.[40] The same expression is used by God in Ezekiel 16:8 when He likens His covenant agreement with Israel to that of a marriage covenant: "I spread the corner of my garment over you and covered your nakedness. I gave you my solemn oath and entered into a covenant with you."

When Ruth requested Boaz to throw his "garment" over her she used the same Hebrew word that is translated "wings" in chapter one. Boaz had prayed that God would reward Ruth because she sought refuge under the "wings" of the God of Israel.[41] It is also the same Hebrew word David used many times in the Psalms to illustrate protection and refuge. A good example is Psalm 57:1,2:

> "... in you my soul takes refuge. I will take refuge in the shadow of your 'wings' until the disaster has passed. I cry out to God Most High, to God, who fulfills His purpose for me"

God is seen to be working in and through Boaz and Ruth to fulfil his purposes. Boaz, who had prayed for Ruth to come under God's "wings" and be rewarded, is now being asked, by the use of the same word "garment", to answer his own prayer.

Boaz understood Ruth's request and had no hesitation in agreeing to all that she asked. As we have already observed, Boaz knew her to be a woman of noble character and God had inclined his heart toward her.

It's significant that Boaz makes reference to Ruth's noble character at this point, because some commentators believe Boaz was involved in sexual relations with Ruth when he asked her to stay at the threshing floor for the night. But both Boaz and Ruth possessed an integrity of character that enabled them to conduct themselves without being ruled by their passions. Naomi had also trusted in their integrity or she would not have suggested that Ruth take such a course of action.

To have had sexual intercourse at the threshing floor would have destroyed Ruth's reputation as a woman of noble character. She was intent on obeying God's laws. In the culture and era in which she lived, that meant sexual purity until a levirate marriage took place.

There is a possibility that a custom may have existed that was recorded centuries later in the Mishnah, which is the written record of the oral conversations of rabbis as they discussed the Mosaic Laws. The custom read: 'if a man was suspected of having intercourse with a Gentile woman he could not perform levirate marriage with her'.[42]

If this was a custom practised in Boaz's day, it would certainly have been an added reason for Boaz's concern to protect Ruth from any suspicion of immoral conduct.

Boaz, aware that Ruth's visit might be misinterpreted, suggested she stay the night and leave early in the morning before she could be recognised.

Set apart for God

How were Ruth and Boaz able to control their passions? They possessed integrity of character because their lives had been set apart for serving God.

Whatever our status, God wants us to be set apart for Himself. Our widowhood and singleness have to be offered to God so that we can refocus on living for Him as His disciples. When we give ourselves wholly to Him, we become whole again.

> To be wholly set apart for God is to be holy; as we often sing...
> I choose to be holy,
> Set apart for you my Master
> Ready to do your will.

Elisabeth Elliot in her book *Passion and Purity* explains:

> 'Holiness means 'wholeness' and comes from the same Greek root as 'hale'–you know, hale and hearty. Healthy. Fulfilled.'[43]

J.I. Packer in his book *Hot Tub Religion* states:

> 'There is no happiness without holiness. Human nature is so made that its fulfillment, contentment, and freedom become realities only as we learn to love, worship, and serve our Maker'.[44]

A close walk with our Maker is where true happiness lies. To seek marriage in order to gain happiness is a false premise. For those of us who have enjoyed a happy first marriage we need to be conscious of the tendency to believe that remarriage is where we regain joy and fulfilment. God wants us to find that satisfaction, first and foremost, in Himself.

Should I remarry? The answer to the question will be dependent on whether remarriage is in God's plan for my future. It will also depend upon whether I desire to be remarried. If I am set apart for service as a disciple of Christ, whatever my status, then I will be in a position for God to work through me to fulfil His purpose for my life. It is God who will arrange circumstances to occur where paths cross and hearts are drawn towards one another.

God's instruction to me is the same as it is for all who desire to follow His plan for their lives:

"Trust in the Lord and do good;
dwell in the land and enjoy safe pasture.
Delight yourself in the Lord and
He will give you the desires of your heart.
Commit your way to the Lord;
trust in him and he will do this"

Psalm 37:3-5

'God knows very well what we need and that all He does is for our good. If we knew how much He loves us, we would always be ready to face life, both its pleasures and its troubles... We must be convinced that our Father is full of love for us and that He only permits trials to come our way for our own good.

Although we seek and love God because of the blessings He has given us, or for those He may give us in the future, let us not stop there. These blessings, as great as they are, will never carry us as near to Him as a simple act of faith does in a time of need or trouble.

Once and for all, let us begin to be His entirely. Let us banish from our heart and soul all that does not reflect Jesus. Let us ask Him for the grace to do this, so that He alone might rule in our hearts.'

Extract from letter written by brother Lawrence a few days before his death on 12 Feb 1691.'the practice of the presence OF GOD' by brother Lawrence (Whitaker House, 1982)

When Ruth came to her mother-in-law, Naomi asked, "How did it go, my daughter?" Then she told her everything Boaz had done for her and added, "He gave me these six measures of barley, saying, 'Don't go back to your mother-in-law empty-handed.'"

Then Naomi said, "Wait, my daughter, until you find out what happens. For the man will not rest until the matter is settled today."

Meanwhile Boaz went up to the town gate and sat there. When the kinsman-redeemer he had mentioned came along, Boaz said, "Come over here, my friend, and sit down." So he went over and sat down.

Boaz took ten of the elders of the town and said, "Sit here," and they did so. Then he said to the kinsman-redeemer, "Naomi, who has come back from Moab, is selling the piece of land that belonged to our brother Elimelech. I thought I should bring the matter to your attention and suggest that you buy it in the presence of these seated here and in the presence of the elders of my people. If you will redeem it, do so. But if you will not, tell me, so I will know. For no one has the right to do it except you, and I am next in line."

"I will redeem it," he said. Then Boaz said, "On the day you buy the land from Naomi and from Ruth the Moabitess, you acquire the dead man's widow, in order to maintain the name of the dead with his property." At this, the kinsman-redeemer said, "Then I cannot redeem it because I might endanger my own estate. You redeem it yourself. I cannot do it."

(Now in earlier times in Israel, for the redemption and transfer of property to become final, one party took off his sandal and gave it to the other. This was the method of legalizing transactions in Israel.)

So the kinsman-redeemer said to Boaz, "Buy it yourself." And he removed his sandal.

Ruth 3:16-4:8

Chapter 9

God's Plan for my Life

As we seek to serve God as His disciple, He will give us a strong desire to follow His leading, His plan and His will. This does not mean that we will cease to have desires and plans of our own. It means that we willingly place our desires and plans under God's control, expecting Him to direct our course.

Proverbs 16:9 tells us: "In his heart a man plans his course, but the Lord determines his steps." Allowing God to determine our steps requires recognition that He understands us better than we do ourselves and that He knows the best and most fruitful pathway for us through this life. He knows how we can best live a Christ-like life, reflecting His character to others.

Naomi and Boaz both had a plan in mind. They had the same objective in view of providing Ruth with another husband. They were also intent on abiding by God's revealed will: the 'levirate' law. Their human planning was not condemned by God because it was in accord with His revealed will. Their actions were covered by prayer for God's blessing and implicit in their prayer was acknowledgment of God's sovereignty.

Before we can act on God's revealed will we need to know what that is. This will mean becoming familiar with God's revealed Word, the Bible. We need to be continually saturated with His wisdom from the Bible. Prayerfully we must rely on the Holy Spirit to reveal His will to us. Only then can we be sure that it is God working in and through us to accomplish His purposes.

The promise is...

> "If the Lord delights in a man's way, he makes his steps firm"
>
> Psalm 37:23

Just how does God make our steps firm?

I have shared with you the experiences of God's love and care during the first month of my stepping out in faith and obedience to write this book. I believe these blessings were confirmation that God was delighting in my way. He was, in fact, making my steps firm. The blessings have not stopped! As I continue to write, God continues to encourage and bless. I feel like David must have felt when he wrote: "I will proclaim your great deeds"... and ... "celebrate your abundant goodness" (Psalm 145:6,7).

During the second month of writing and after receiving several monetary gifts, I decided to set aside a certain amount of money for a missionary family. My purpose in relating this is not to tell of my giving but to emphasise God's incredible goodness and to illustrate that we never seem to be able to outgive God.

Having written the cheque out in the morning I thought nothing more about it until Michelle, my eldest daughter, returned home that evening from her part-time job. She was carrying two large shopping bags full of towels and sheets. The drapery shop where she worked had supplied a hotel with towels and because of a small fault they had returned them. We had been given ten large bath towels and the same quantity of hand towels and face cloths. Not only were they of excellent quality with most having no fault in them, but they were pink! This was significant because I had only recently re-wallpapered our bathroom and pink was the colour of towels that I needed.

Rachael, my younger daughter, who had moved to another city at the beginning of the year in order to further her education, was also in need of towels. She was able to rejoice with us for God's provision as we shared some of the towels with her.

In the other bag were three pairs of single sheets and a double sheet. These were the best quality cotton sheets and sold at $54.95 for a single sheet. Michelle had been given the opportunity of purchasing them for $5 a pair, simply because they had not sold in the sale. Because she had bought them she was given a double sheet free. I marvelled at God's goodness. Only the previous day I had mentioned to Michelle that I was in need of another double sheet. Not only did God provide the best quality sheets but once more He provided the right colours to match our bed-covers! No wonder David exclaimed:

"The Lord is... rich in love" Psalm 145:8

The following month God provided the money for my younger daughter Rachael and my son Andrew to attend Easter Camp. Through the generosity of a Christian couple, I was given a painting which I had admired for some time. God was continually making my steps firm, for He not only provided for my needs but my wants as well! He continues to display His abundant goodness to us in many different ways.

God who had allowed our sorrow was assuring us that we could depend upon Him to provide and care for us. He was showing us, as Jesus taught, that if we first seek His kingdom and His righteousness then all these "things" we need will be "given" to us. He was reminding us not to worry about the future: "Therefore do not worry about tomorrow, for tomorrow will worry about itself. Each day has enough trouble of its own" (Matt 6:34).

God promises that if we live to please Him, He will provide our daily needs. He also promises to guide us in our pathway through life. Often He only allows us to see one step ahead. This is good because it causes us to be constantly dependent upon Him. God wants us to draw closer to Him, exercising our faith as we seek His guidance.

He does not lead me year by year
Nor even day by day.
But step by step my path unfolds;
My Lord directs my way.

Tomorrow's plan I do not know,
I only know this minute;
But He will say, " This is the way,
By faith now walk ye in it."

And I am glad that it is so.
Today's enough to bear;
And when tomorrow comes, His grace
Shall far exceed its care.

What need to worry then, or fret?
The God who gave His Son
Holds all my moments in His hand
And gives them, one by one.

Anon

Waiting on God

When Ruth returned home and told Naomi what had happened at the threshing floor, Naomi instructed her to wait and see what would happen. Naomi was confident that God would act on behalf of Ruth and Boaz. Ruth, who in faith had asked Boaz to fulfil the special conditions of a 'levirate' marriage, was content to wait. She trusted God to fulfil His purposes for her. Boaz, who had promised to do all he could to comply with Ruth's proposal, also acknowledged that it was God who would work out His purposes through him.

To "be still before the Lord" and to "wait patiently for Him" (Psa 37:7) can sometimes be a very hard thing to do! Living in our modern Western world of instant 'everything' makes it even harder to exercise patience. We flick a switch and have instant light. We can flick another switch and have instant heat for cooking or warmth. With a flick of the wrist the tap is turned and we get instant hot water. Microwaves cook our dinners in seconds. We have instant TV dinners, instant puddings, instant noodles and often demand instant answers!

Why is it that God requires us to wait patiently for Him? I believe the answer is twofold.

Firstly, God wants us to learn to trust in Him with our whole being. He doesn't want us to rely on our own understanding! In Proverbs 3:5-6 we are told:

> "Trust in the Lord with all your heart and lean not on your own understanding; in all your ways acknowledge him, and he will make your paths straight."

The second reason why God sometimes requires us to wait is because His timing is different to ours (Hab 2:3). The apostle Paul learnt that God's timing is perfect.

In Romans 1:13 we are told that Paul planned many times to go to Rome but was hindered from going. His plans were in accordance with God's will but the timing was wrong. God knew the right time for Paul to be in Rome in order to gain the greatest number of converts.

Waiting on God is not exactly passive. It is a living faith that believes that God will act. It involves faith and trust. Trusting Him means relying on His faithfulness. It involves the same of us today, as it has for many of God's people throughout history. We are to trust in the Lord, do good, enjoy our present state, delight in the Lord, commit our way to Him, not fret and refrain from anger (Psalm 37:3-8). This requires an attitude of patience, which in turn matures us in Christ (James 1:3,4).

God wants us to tell Him about our plans and to talk them over with Him. He expects us to act on His revealed will and to trust Him for the courage to perform it.

To tell God about ourselves and our difficulties yet continue to have fears and anxiety, is not really trusting God. We are looking at our circumstances instead of placing our complete confidence in Him.

The Lord gives the following promises to those who learn to trust Him and wait for Him to act:

- our strength will be renewed (Isa 40:31)
- courage and guidance will be given (Psa 37:23,24,34)
- peace will be enjoyed (Psa 37: 9,11)
- the desires of our heart will be given (Psa 37: 3,4)
- He will act righteously on our behalf (Lam 3:24-26).

Not only is our faith exercised and stretched as we wait but so is our patience. As someone has said, 'God seldom does great things in a hurry. Yet He has never been known to disappoint those whose expectation is from Him'.

> "My soul, wait silently for God alone, for my expectation is from him"
>
> Psalm 62:5 (NKJV)

Waiting in darkness

Sometimes the future looks dark. Many experience a cloud of darkness and depression following the death of their partner. There seems to be no way out of the fog. It feels impossible to go on. Despite our circumstances, God wants us to cling to Him alone, not to one's self or any other person. When David wrote, "wait silently for God alone," it was during a time when his heart's cry was directed to God and his expectation was from Him alone.

Isaiah also described this darkness as a time when we are to trust in God and wait on Him: "Who among you fears the Lord? Who obeys the voice of His servant? Who walks in darkness, and has no light? Let him trust in the name of the Lord, and rely upon his God" (Isa 50:10 NKJV). God is the only one who can bring us out of this darkness.

Several years ago I found myself in a situation which I likened in my diary to a darkened waiting room with no windows or doors! I had been involved in three specific areas of service for the Lord and because of various circumstances it became necessary for me to leave each position. The three doors of service closed within a few weeks of each other. This left me in a place of darkness wondering what God was doing! Perplexed and discouraged, I waited in my dark fog.

For six weeks I prayed, read God's Word and waited patiently for redirection. One night as I was playing the piano and singing the old hymn 'I Am Thine O Lord', the lines of the second verse spoke to me. . .

Consecrate me now to thy service Lord
By the power of grace divine,
Let my soul look up with steadfast hope,
And my will be lost in thine.

It was as if I suddenly saw a ray of light in the darkness. Although God had shut these areas of service in which I had been so busy, He was reminding me of an area of His will I had neglected. He once again convicted me to return to my writing. *This was the door that was already open* but I had turned my back on it because of my involvement in other legitimate good works.

About that time I was reading J.I. Packer's book, *Hot Tub Religion,* when the following words struck a chord within my heart: 'the irreverence of not obeying the guidance you have received already, will act as atmospherics in one's heart, making recognition of God's will harder than it should be. . .'[45] As I once again took up writing seriously as a priority, God in His own special way, reopened one of the doors of service in which I had been previously involved.

Waiting together in prayer

The two widows, Ruth and Naomi, waited before God together. It is good when two can come together and wait before God in prayer, as might a husband and wife. As a widow I have found great value in the prayer support of others; whether it be another widow, a friend or a church counsellor. It is essential to spend time alone with God but it is also good to ask others to pray with and for us.

Paul asked the Christians at Ephesus to pray for him and exhorted them to pray for one another (Eph 6:18,19). Along with Silas and Timothy, he constantly prayed for the Christians at Thessalonica:

> "... we constantly pray for you, that our God... by his power he may fulfill every good purpose of yours and every act prompted by your faith"
>
> 2 Thess 1:11

I have this verse pinned up on my wall above my word processor as an encouragement to keep writing. It is a reminder to me that God is at work, fulfilling His purposes through me. It is encouraging to know that others are praying for me.

God does not expect us to be an island unto ourselves! He does not want us to live lonely, single lives, independent of others. It is not, as I had grown-up believing, a sign of weakness to ask others to pray for us. Christians are exhorted repeatedly throughout the New Testament to pray for one another, to comfort one another and to support one another. If for some reason a widow does not receive this kind of support that she so desperately needs, she may well become engulfed in a cloud of despondency and loneliness.

I was speaking to a friend just recently who told me that when widowed some years ago, not one person from the church she attended talked to her about her husband's death. No-one had visited to comfort or pray with her. She was treated as if no tragedy had occurred. It was as if her husband had never even existed!

Unfortunately the lack of support which the women of Bethlehem displayed towards Ruth and Naomi on their return to the city is the same reaction some widows receive today. The reason for the silence and lack of comforters could simply be that many just don't know what to say. They decide to stay away from the bereaved to avoid any embarrassment. Some even reason that God is punishing the couple because of some supposed past sin.

Many lack an understanding of the difference between the suffering of the wicked as punishment and the suffering of the righteous to accomplish God's higher purposes. Instead of acting as Job's friends who verbally passed judgment or like the women of Bethlehem who silently passed judgment, it is much more encouraging to experience love and kindness from others. This was the attitude God displayed towards Ruth and Naomi–an attitude of loving-kindness which was beautifully reflected in the actions of Boaz towards the two widows.

When death occurs and we are crushed, broken-hearted and vulnerable, we need the love and support of other Christians and family. If this encouragement is not received loneliness ensues, resulting in a lengthening of the grieving process.

Loneliness

The widowed list loneliness as a major problem. Loneliness is more pronounced for the widowed than the divorced, separated or single. This is because death instantaneously deprives one of their loving companion. The resulting void is a desert of loneliness.

We must not feel guilty about experiencing this loneliness. It is a normal part of grieving for the companionship that was once shared. God created in us the fundamental need to give love and receive it and to experience the body-soul relationship of marriage. It is God's solution to the problem of loneliness. In the garden of Eden, when He surveyed His creation, God said: "It is not good for the man to be alone," and created a suitable companion for him.

We must be careful not to dwell on our loneliness. This will result in self-pity, which if allowed to grow, will result in bitterness towards God and others. The writer of Hebrews advises: "See to it that. . . no bitter root grows up to cause trouble and defile many" (Heb 12:15).

A way out

In the midst of my grief, I wrote in the front of my Bible these words from Psalm 10:14, which I saw as three forward steps:

> "But you, O God, do *see* trouble and grief;
> you *consider* it to take it in hand.
> The victim *commits* himself to you."

It is important to recognise that nothing escapes the eye of God! He knows our grief and wants to be with us in it. He wants to deliver us from it but first we must give ourselves and our grief to Him.

I believe the way out of the desert of loneliness involves more than this. For me, the way out was the surrender of myself in my grief, to a loving Father whose reasoning I could not understand. This was a simple trust in the character of God who is love, a God who did not want to harm me but desired my highest good. This is beautifully expressed in the chorus:

> Don't you know that I love you?
> Before you were born I knew you.
> Don't you know that my plans for you are good?
> Look and see I've engraved you on the palms of my hands;
> Look and see I've engraved you on my hands.

During this desert experience I gained much comfort from prayerfully reading through the Psalms. I am thankful for David's honesty before God! He openly expressed his desperation, loneliness, sorrow and anger, yet always found his joy restored by concentrating on the character of God. I underlined the words *"his love"* and *"his faithfulness"* when David repeatedly drew strength from meditating on these aspects of God's character.

I allowed myself to refocus on the character of God and to meditate on His love and faithfulness. I thought of how He had displayed these attributes to both of us throughout the time of Alan's illness and death. I realised that God's love and faithfulness were immovable. I felt like the prophet Jeremiah who many years ago wrote:

> "I remember my affliction and my wandering, the bitterness and the gall. I well remember them, and my soul is downcast within me. Yet this I call to mind and therefore I have hope: Because of the Lord's great love we are not consumed, for his compassions never fail. They are new every morning; great is your faithfulness"
>
> Lam 3:19-23

With the focus off myself and upon God's character, I found my love for Him grew stronger. As I drew closer to Him, the warmth of His love caused the icy fingers of loneliness to melt. This resulted in a greater capacity to share His love with others.

Elisabeth Elliot in her book *The Path of Loneliness* sums it up this way:

> '...the answer to loneliness is love, not our finding someone to love us, but our surrendering to the God who has always loved us with an everlasting love. Loving Him is then expressed in a happy and full-hearted pouring out of ourselves in love to others.' [46]

Richard Foster refers to the inner emptiness of loneliness being overcome by cultivating an inner solitude. He believes this inner solitude of mind and heart alone with God will produce outward manifestations where:

'. . . we can never again pass off lightly the quiet depression and sad loneliness of those we meet. We become one with all who hurt and are afraid. We are free to give them the greatest gift we possess: the gift of ourselves.' [47]

Paul reminds us in 2 Corinthians 1:3,4 that because we have received comfort from the "Father of compassion" and the "God of all comfort" in the time of our trouble, we are able to similarly comfort others in their time of trouble. This is beautifully expressed in Janet Fleming's poem *A Glowing Pearl*:

A glowing pearl would never be
So beautiful for one to see,
Had not an oyster known the pain
Caused by the piercing of sand's grain.

The kauri tall that reaches high
And grows as if to reach the sky;
Could never make such lovely wood
If it had not life's storms withstood.

A diamond bright upon a hand
That shines beside a wedding band,
As sparkling bright would never gleam
Had it not formed within earth's seams.

The twinkling star which shines by night
In darkest hours will beam most bright,
To bring a ray of hope to one
Who waits the rising of the sun.

For gems of character that bless,
Like kindness, love and gentleness,
Or patience and humility,
Aren't gained through ease, but 'tragedy'.

As scented leaves upon a tree
When crushed will smell more fragrantly,
So may the hurts I bear today
In future bless another's way.

Ruth and Naomi supported each other in whatever way they could. They loved each other with a pure and selfless love. Ruth, the younger widow, was able to do the physical things that perhaps her older mother-in-law found difficult. No doubt, they discussed their problems and prayed over them together.

It has been of tremendous value to me to meet with other widows on a monthly lunch date for some years now, just to share thoughts, discuss our feelings and problems and sometimes pray together.

Groups have been set up specifically to support widows and widowers who are grieving and suffering loneliness. THEOS is one such group, based in Pittsburgh and spread throughout the United States and Canada. THEOS, the Greek word for God, is also an acronym for They Help Each Other Spiritually. For contact write to THEOS Foundation, 717 Liberty Avenue, 1301 Clark Bldg, Pittsburgh, Pennsylvania 15222.

Romans 8:28,29 teaches us that God's purposes in allowing trials and sufferings in our lives is for our good, so that we might become more Christ-like: "... to be conformed to the likeness of His Son." If we grasp hold of this truth it will help us accept the adverse circumstances God allows to occur in our lives. It is part of His plan to draw us closer to Himself. As J.I. Packer explains:

'The "good" for which all things work is not the immediate ease and comfort of God's children (as is, one fears, too often supposed), but their ultimate holiness and conformity to the likeness of Christ'.[48]

The ultimate purpose is to bring glory to God Himself.

> "In him we were also chosen, having been predestined according to the plan of him who works out everything in conformity with the purpose of his will, in order that we, who were the first to hope in Christ, might be for the praise of his glory"
>
> Eph 1:11,12

Waiting for God's choice

For Ruth and Naomi this was a time of waiting patiently at home and allowing God to act in the hearts of others. God is always active on behalf of those who seek to do His revealed will, who prayerfully wait, trusting Him to fulfil His purposes.

> "God... who acts on behalf of those who wait for him"
>
> Isaiah 64:4

Boaz, who had a plan in mind was also subject to God's revealed will: the 'levirate' law. This required the closest male relative of the deceased to purchase his land and marry his widow.

Ruth and Naomi seemed unaware of the existence of a closer relative than Boaz but Boaz knew of him and sought to honour God's law. The city gate was the ideal place to locate him as everyone had to pass through that gate en route to fields, threshing floor and other cities. It was the place where the townsfolk gathered for conversation and administration of justice. It was also where business and legal transactions took place and the poor waited for aid.[49]

As Boaz had anticipated, his relative soon came along. He took him aside to talk with him. In the correct legal manner he chose ten elders to act as witnesses to his conversation. He told him of Naomi's need to sell the land which belonged to Elimelech and reminded him that as the nearest relative, he had the right of purchase. The relative's positive response exposed his greed. Financially, it would have been a good deal as Naomi had no heirs and she was too old to produce an heir to inherit the land!

After gaining such a positive response, Boaz then informed the nearer kinsman of a fact he appeared not to know. When he purchased the land from Naomi he would also have to buy the land from"Ruth *the Moabitess*!" This would also mean marrying Ruth!

At this, his response changed to a definite "NO!" He knew that if a 'levirate' son was born to Ruth, the property would revert to her child and he would lose the purchase money plus the land. His selfishness was exposed. He was interested only in his own gain, his own property and his own name. He was not the right man for Ruth!

There was a dramatic contrast in attitude between this man and Boaz. The financial cost was unimportant to Boaz. He was prepared to lay aside the importance of his own possessions and name. As previously mentioned, a mutual love and respect had developed between Ruth and Boaz. Boaz desired Ruth's highest good to the point of considerable self-sacrifice.

God had prepared the hearts and lives of these two very ordinary people so they would meet at the right time. Many of us struggle with impatience and find it difficult to be still and wait patiently for the Lord to act.

Throughout the Bible, when God's people struggled with impatience He repeatedly told them to "remember." Psalm 106 recalls how God's people fell into sin because they "did not remember your many kindnesses" (v7), ". . . they soon forgot what he had done and did not wait for His counsel" (v13).

Earlier, I described how God provided us with towels and sheets of the right colour. If God is interested in such details, surely I can trust Him to be concerned with the other more important details in my life. He is the one who knows my deepest needs and He will meet those needs out of His abundance. In His own good time He may even provide the right man to be my husband! As pieces of a jigsaw puzzle are shaped and honed to perfectly fit together to form a whole picture, so God prepares each one of us. He has a plan and

"... works out everything in conformity with the purpose of His will" (Eph 1:11).

Then Boaz announced to the elders and all The people, "Today you are witnesses that I have bought from Naomi all the property of Elimelech, Kilion and Mahlon. I have also acquired Ruth the Moabitess, Mahlon's widow, as my wife, in order to maintain the name of the dead with his property, so that his name will not disappear from among his family or from the town records. Today you are witnesses!"

Then the elders and all those at the gate said, "We are witnesses. May the Lord make the woman who is coming into your home like Rachel and Leah, who together built up the house of Israel. May you have standing in Ephrathah and be famous in Bethlehem. Through the offspring the Lord gives you by this young woman, may your family be like that of Perez, whom Tamar bore to Judah."

So Boaz took Ruth and she became his wife. Then he went to her, and the Lord enabled her to conceive, and she gave birth to a son. The women said to Naomi: "Praise be to the Lord, who this day has not left you without a kinsman-redeemer. May he become famous throughout Israel! He will renew your life and sustain you in your old age. For your daughter-in-law, who loves you and who is better to you than seven sons, has given him birth."

Then Naomi took the child, laid him in her lap and cared for him. The women living there said, "Naomi has a son." And they named him Obed. He was the father of Jesse, the father of David.

Ruth 4:9-17

Chapter 10

Triumphant

What an incredible plan God had in mind for these two destitute widows. Why were they included in His plan? What made Ruth so special that God should choose her to be in the lineage of Christ? How did Ruth and Naomi come to be in a position to fulfil God's purposes? How did they actually become women of influence for God?

The answer to these questions lies in the simple fact that both Ruth and Naomi chose of their own free will, to love and obey God despite their circumstances. As they sought to follow His revealed will, He was able to work through them to fulfil His purposes. He delighted in abundantly blessing them.

Has God a plan in mind for me? Am I special to Him? If so, how can I make sure that I am in a position where God can work out His purposes through me? How can I become a woman of influence for God today?

Highlighted in this last chapter of the book of Ruth is the principle that God graciously rewards those who faithfully follow Him and obey His word. Just as Ruth and Naomi made a conscious decision to love God and follow His ways, we also need to make a conscious decision to love God with our whole heart and obey His revealed will. He has a plan and purpose for each of our lives and desires to work through us and to richly bless us.

The younger widow

Frank Slaughter, in his novel *The Song of Ruth*, depicts Ruth as 'a young girl of about twenty' who was 'startingly beautiful, with dark red hair, high cheekbones, and warm eyes.'[50] However, the biblical account gives no description of Ruth's appearance and although she was obviously a lot younger than Boaz, one is left guessing as to her exact age. The author of the book of Ruth wants us to be drawn, as was Boaz and the people of Bethlehem, to her character and not her appearance. They referred to her as "a woman of noble character" who was good and kind to her widowed mother-in-law.

Ruth put aside her former way of life as a Moabite who worshipped many gods and chose to live and serve the God of Israel. As a loving daughter-in-law she showed a genuineness which reflected to others the character of a loving God.

Paul reminds us that whether young, old, widowed, single, married or whatever, we are to display to others His character of righteousness, holiness and sacrificial love.

"... with regard to your former way of life, put off your old self... be made new in the attitude of your minds; and put on the new self, created to be like God in true righteousness and holiness... Be imitators of God, therefore, as dearly loved children and live a life of love, just as Christ loved us and gave himself up for us as a fragrant offering and sacrifice to God"

Eph 4:22-24; 5:1-2

The elders and witnesses at the town gate had no hesitation in praying for a blessing on the marriage union between Boaz and Ruth. They knew Ruth's character and knew she loved and served the same God as Boaz. They prayed that the marriage might be blessed with children, desiring Ruth to be like Rachel and Leah from whom descended the entire nation of Israel.

These elders acknowledged that it is God who is the giver of life and that children are a gift from Him. When Obed was conceived this was attributed directly to God: *"the Lord* enabled her to conceive." Later when he was born, the women of Bethlehem praised the Lord for the gift of a son. What a contrast with those today who cry out for the right of abortion! They are in fact, crying out against God's right to give life! (Psa 127:3; 139:13-16; Eccl 11:5; Jer 1:5)

After only a few months in Bethlehem, Ruth became known as a woman of integrity and great kindness. At the birth of her son, the same women who had been silent when she entered Bethlehem, now exalted and praised her as "better to Naomi than seven sons." What a striking tribute! Ruth probably received the highest praise a woman could gain in a society which considered sons–not daughters–of great importance (1 Sam 2:5).

Choosing to walk by faith

Ruth *chose to live out* her widowhood endeavouring to obey God's revealed will and living a life of sacrificial love. When she set out on the journey to Bethlehem, Ruth could have thought of her own security and returned to Moab but she *chose instead to protect* and provide for her old, widowed mother-in-law.

Ruth *chose to go and work* in the reaping fields, trusting in the laws of God for the provision of grain for the widow. The 'levirate' marriage had been Naomi's suggestion but Ruth *chose to obey* because it was God's law. Her uppermost thought was not one of benefiting herself, but of benefiting her mother-in-law.

Ruth epitomises what Paul describes as the attitude that should characterise a follower of Christ. She had to "find out what pleases the Lord" and "understand what the Lord's will is" (Eph 5:10,17). Ruth chose to look to the interests of others and did nothing out of selfish ambition. In humility she considered others better than herself (Phil 2:2-5).

God has created us with a free will. *We* choose whether or not we follow Him. God challenges us, as Joshua challenged the Israelites: "Choose for yourselves this day whom you will serve" (Josh 24:15).

During my first year of study at Bible College of New Zealand a need arose for someone to type lecturers' notes. I chose to respond to that need. Helping in this way led to secretarial involvement for a number of years. This was followed by two years as Office Secretary which included administrative and librarian work.

In 1993 God impressed upon my mind and heart the need to write this book. In response *I chose to leave* my secretarial job in order to concentrate on writing. Later in the year when I had finished the draft copy the Lord opened a door of service in an area of work I was already involved in. I had been helping in open-air evangelism in the streets of Wellington for a year when a need arose in the Wellington Branch of OAC Ministries for an Office Manager. After seeking the Lord's guidance *I chose to obey* His leading and over the past year I have enjoyed working in a place where God is continually opening many and varied doors to work and witness for Him.

Over the past seven years God has continually guided and directed my steps, just as He did for Ruth and Naomi. The pathway has not always been easy but the choice to walk that path has always been mine.

Ruth was blessed beyond her wildest dreams because she chose to trust in God and obey His revealed will. Although she experienced much blessing from God, Ruth like Job, never fully understood or saw in her lifetime the far reaching effects of her faith and obedience. God's plans and purposes were far beyond what she could grasp... "As the heavens are higher than the earth, so are my ways higher than your ways and my thoughts than your thoughts" (Isa 55:9).

Ruth walked by faith. God did not tell Ruth, while she was a destitute foreign widow, that she would be accepted by God's people as one with them. At that time He did not reveal to her that she would be loved by an Israelite of influence and wealth, who would eventually marry her, or that He would bless her with a son!

Ruth lived in an era when Israel was ruled by judges and had never had a king to rule over them. It was therefore impossible for her to comprehend that her son would become the grandfather of King David and in the lineage of Christ, the Messiah.

Ruth acted in faith, trusting in a good God whom she believed desired her highest good. God's plans for her good were far far greater than her understanding or expectations and so too, are His plans for you and me. Many of us will never know in our lifetime the full extent of God's purposes as He works through us. One day in eternity we may see and understand.

Ruth was greatly blessed with a happy second marriage. It is important however, to realise she had not sought remarriage as an escape from widowhood! She had not sought remarriage as an answer to her desire for happiness. If these are the motives behind our desire for remarriage then there will remain a void in our lives because God wants us to find our deepest satisfaction in Him. This is not found to the same extent in anybody else! Ruth had been content to serve God in whatever way He led, whether that meant living out her days providing for Naomi and remaining single, or whether it meant remarriage in obedience to the 'levirate' law. She had "learned to be content *whatever the circumstances*" (Phil 4:11).

The older widow

What of Naomi, the older widow? Was she too old for God to work out His purposes through her? Did He bless her beyond her expectations? Is this same God able to work through the older widow today and bless her?

Naomi returned to Bethlehem with no sons or grandchildren to inherit Elimelech's land and no-one to carry on the family name but she soon discovered that God had not left her. He remained faithful to this lonely, destitute and grieving widow. We saw earlier from the Old Testament lament that Naomi held on to a God she could not understand but she acknowledged that her life was under His control. Although she could see no answers to her dilemma she trusted God to deliver her.

Are you hurting, sad and lonely,
Is your life one load of cares?
God can help you bear your burden
Turn your trials into prayers.

Sickness, hunger, pain, bereavement,
Poverty have come your way;
Though you weep in life's dark midnight
Hope can view a bright new day.[51]

The author of Ruth has delight in telling us that 'a bright new day' would dawn for Naomi! Indeed, Naomi's prayers were fulfilled through her daughter-in-law, whom she had overlooked when she thought she had returned to Bethlehem empty.

We can be so caught up with our problems and sufferings that we cannot see how God can ever bring any good out of them. But God always has a plan! In His gracious compassion for this suffering widow God supplied her immediate temporal needs. He provided her with the companionship of Ruth to alleviate her loneliness. When Naomi sought to alleviate Ruth's loneliness, she too was blessed beyond her wildest expectations. She was blessed with a grandson.

Many of Naomi's needs were met with the birth of Obed. The women of Bethlehem said: "He will renew your life and sustain you in your old age." Obed would become heir to the property that Boaz had purchased, therefore he would be able to sustain and support Naomi as she grew older. In Proverbs 17:6 we are told: "Children's children are a crown to the aged."

Naomi, like Ruth, could never have fully understood the extent of God's purposes when the women prayed that Obed "may become famous throughout Israel." She could not have comprehended that her obedience to God and Ruth's marriage to Boaz, would result in Obed being in the lineage of Christ.

We are never too old to be useful to God. I was greatly challenged by an address given by an older widow at a recent weekend retreat. The sprightly eighty year old told of how she and her husband obeyed God's call to foreign mission and served fifteen years in Bolivia and thirty-five years in Paraguay bringing the Good News to many people. She had returned to New Zealand as a widow, her husband having died five years earlier. Now she felt useless. In deep exercise of heart and mind she cried out to God because she did not want to be an *'armchair vegetable'*. She asked Him to make her availability worthwhile and to use her in some way.

God took her at her word and what amazing experiences this disciple of Christ told. God used her firstly in the conversion of her neighbours and they in turn, became dedicated Christians reaching out to many others. She shared how she sought to reach the teenagers in the area in which she lived by making her home available to them. The first night she invited them to watch a video of the life of Jesus and twenty-five teenagers arrived. Five were converted that night. She continues to show the love of Christ to many who are rejected by society and family. Homosexuals, aids victims, rapists and drug addicts. Many of these have come to know Christ as their Saviour. She is currently running a weekly Bible study with these new

Christians. Her challenge was: *be available to the Lord!*

In hindsight we are privileged to read and observe something of God's dealings in the lives of Ruth and Naomi. We are able to see that although He had a plan for their lives, He allowed them to make choices. They suffered the death of their spouses but God permitted these circumstances to occur for their good and left the responses to them. Similarly, many of us have suffered the death of our spouse but God wants to bring good out of our circumstances. If we respond in faith and make ourselves available to Him, He will work through us for our ultimate good. In so doing, this should bring blessing to others as well!

As you look back over this last paragraph it may seem rather pious. I want to emphasise that I am not saying that the Christian who is suffering should be joyful and glibly say, '. . . all things happen for the good of those who love the Lord!' I have heard too many well-meaning comforters misquote Romans 8:28 in this way. This is not what the verse is saying. It says: "And we know that in all things God works for the good of those who love him." It is a promise that God will ultimately turn our tragedies into triumphs if we trust Him. For me this has been a painful pathway. In Hebrews 12 it says that hardship is to be seen as discipline:

"Endure hardship as discipline"
. . . because. . .
"God disciplines us for our good"
. . . and. . .
"No discipline seems pleasant at the time,
but painful."

The promise that follows is: "Later on, however it produces a harvest of righteousness and peace for those who have been trained by it" (v7,10,11).

God desires to richly bless us as He did for Ruth and Naomi. Paul reminds us to be:

> "like slaves of Christ, doing the will of God from your heart. Serve wholeheartedly. . . because you know that the Lord will reward everyone for whatever good he does."
>
> ". . . for it is God who works in you to will and act according to his good purpose."
>
> Eph 6:6-8; Phil 2:13

If we do the will of God from our heart, seeking to serve Him wholeheartedly in whatever area of work He has led us, then He promises to bless. We should not seek to please God in order to receive a reward. Rewards and blessings come as a result of a positive relationship with God, coupled with constant obedience to Him.

Ruth, the Gentile widow and Naomi, the Israelite widow, were both accepted by God–not because of any acts of righteousness which they did but simply because they placed their faith and trust in Him. Today, God operates on the same principle. He accepts anyone who makes the decision to place their personal faith and trust in Him.

We are not accepted because of any righteous works we may have done, for "the righteousness from God comes through faith in Jesus Christ to all who believe" (Rom 3:22)... "there is no difference between Jew and Gentile, the same Lord is Lord of all and richly blesses all who call on Him" (Rom 10:12).

Job said of God: "I know that you can do all things: no plan of yours can be thwarted" (Job 42:2). God watched over the family line through which his Son would be born into the world. Through the dark days of the judges He chose two faithful widows to play an important role in that lineage.

This same God has a plan and a purpose for your life and mine.

> "For I know the plans I have for you", declares the Lord, "plans to prosper you and not to harm you, plans to give you hope and a future"
>
> Jer 29:11

God requires the same of us today, as He did of Ruth and Naomi who lived in a different culture, many thousands of years ago.

- We must "live as children of light (for the fruit of the light consists in all goodness, righteousness and truth) and find out what pleases the Lord" (Eph 5: 8-10).
- We must consciously choose to trust and obey a good God, making ourselves avail-

able for His service. To "live a life of love. . . as a fragrant offering and sacrifice to God" (Eph 5:2).

- We must learn to be content whatever our circumstances and "do everything through Him who gives us strength." God's promise is that He will meet all our needs "according to his glorious riches in Christ Jesus" (Phil 4:11,13,19).

This is amazing, for His glorious and unfathomable riches can never end.

THE WEAVER

My life is but a weaving between my Lord and me.
I may not choose the colours, He knows what they should be,
For He can view the pattern upon the upper side,
While I can see it only on this the under side.
Sometimes He weaveth sorrow which seemeth strange to me,
But I will trust His judgment and work on faithfully,
'Tis He who fills the shuttle, He knows just what is best
So I will weave in earnest and leave with Him the rest.
Not 'til the loom is silent, and the shuttles cease to fly,
Will God unroll the canvas, and explain the reason why.
The dark threads are as needful in the Weaver's skilful hand,
As the threads of gold and silver in the pattern He has planned.

(Author unknown)

Notes

Chapter 1:

1. Exodus 22:22-24; Deuteronomy 24:17; Isaiah 1:17; Jeremiah 22:3; Zechariah 7:10; Proverbs 15:25.
2. Exodus 23:10-11 cf Leviticus 25:1-7; Deuteronomy 14:28,29; 24:19-21; 26:12-13.
3. Exodus 22:22-24; Psalms 109:9, Isaiah 47:8-9; Jeremiah 15:8; Lamentations 5:3.

Chapter 2:

4. D.Atkinson, The Message of Ruth : The Bible Speaks Today (IVP 1983) pp34-35.
5. E.Smick, Job : *The Expositors Bible Commentary* (Zondervan 1988) p1056.
6. ibid p884.
7. Mary Moster, *Living with Cancer :NICOT* (Eerdmans 1988) p96.

Chapter 3:

8. K.Wiebe, *Alone : Through Widowhood and Beyond–A Search for Joy* (Hodder & Stoughton 1987) p13.

Chapter 4:

9. Claus Westermann, 'The Role of the Lament in the Theology of the Old Testament' (Interpretation 28, 1974).
10. Genesis 38:14; 2 Samuel 12:20; 14:2; Isaiah 61:3; Daniel 10:3.

11. *Encyclopedia Britannica* Vol 7
(W & H Benton 1973-4) p98.
12. Elisha - 2 Kings 8:11; Joseph - Genesis 43:30;
David - Psalm 102:9; 2 Samuel 12:22; 15:30; 18:33.
13. Psalm 78:64; Job 27:13-15.
14. Malachi 3:16.

Chapter 5:
15. V. Austin, C.Clarke-Smith (Editors),
Widowed - What now? (Mallinson Rendel NZ)
Quote from Ch 2 "The Stages of Grief"
by Dr Richard Turnbull, pp30-31.
16. ibid p31.

Chapter 6:
17. R.L.Hubbard Jr, The Book of Ruth *NICOT*
(Eerdmans 1988) p179.
18. B.Decker, *After the Flowers Have Gone*
(Zondervan 1980) pp66-67.
19. J.W.Wenham, T*he Elements of NT Greek*
(Cambridge 1967) p27.
20. W.E.Vine, *Expository Dictionary of NT Words*
(Oliphants 1940) pp38-39.
21. Deuteronomy 25:5-6.

Chapter 7:
22. Deuteronomy 10:18; Psalm 68:5; 146:9
23. T.F. Jones, *Sex & Love when you're Single Again*
(Oliver-Nelson 1990) p102.
24. Genesis 24:34-38; Judges 14:2-10.

25. D.R.Pape, *In Search of God's Ideal Woman*
(IVP 1977) p254.
26. N.K. Johnson, *Alone and Beginning Again*
(Judson 1982) p111.
27. B.Decker, *After the Flowers Have Gone*
(Zondervan 1980) p154.
28. Hosea 2:1-3:5; Jeremiah 31:31-32.
29. R.A.Watson, Judges and Ruth :*The Expositor's Bible*
(Hodder & Stoughton 1980) p392.
30. C.J.Barber, *A Story of God's Grace : Ruth*
(Moody 1983) p96.
31. Extract from poem by Janet Fleming, *Perhaps the Hardest Thing of All*

Chapter 8:
32. J.B.Hurley, *Man and Woman in Biblical Perspective*
(Zondervan 1981) p97 quoting Rabbi Hillel, and p65
Mishnah (mKet.7.6).
33. ibid p63, quoting rabbi Eliezer's statement
(bYom.66b).
34. ibid p62, quoting rabbi Judah ben Elai (bMen.43b).
35. R.Earle, 1, 2 Timothy : *The Expositor's Bible*
Commentary (Zondervan 1978)p378.
36. J.B.Hurley, *Man and Woman in Biblical Perspective*
(Zondervan 1981) p137.
37. D.Pape, *In Search of God's Ideal Woman*
(IVP 1977) p253.
38. NIV Study Bible Notes p1732.

39. J.M.Freeman, *Manners and Customs of the Bible* (Logos 1972) Item 245, p129.
40. L.Morris, Judges and Ruth : *Tyndale OT Commentaries* (IVP 1968) Note 1 p289, quoting statement by Tabari.
41. M.Gow, 'Prayer and Providence in the Book of Ruth'
(CBRF Journal, Jan 1985) p15.
42. L.Morris, Judges and Ruth :*Tyndale OT Commentaries* (IVP 1968) pp293-4,
quoting the Mishnah (Yeb.2:8).
43. E.Elliot, *Passion and Purity* (Revell 1984) p41.
44. J.I.Packer, *Hot Tub Religion* (Tyndale 1988) p176.

Chapter 9:
45. J.I.Packer, *Hot Tub Religion* (Tyndale 1988) pp129-130.
46. E.Elliot, *The Path of Loneliness* (Kingsway 1990) p158.
47. R.Foster, Study Guide for *Celebration of Discipline*
(Hodder & Stoughton1983) p57.
48. J.I.Packer, *Hot Tub Religion* (Tyndale 1988) pp33,34.
49. D.Atkinson, The Message of Ruth (IVP 1983) p110.

Chapter 10:

50. F.G. Slaughter, *The Song of Ruth* (Panther 1960) pp15,22.

51. Extract from poem by Janet Fleming, *Are You Hurting.*